Bookcraft

Bookcraft

Techniques for Binding, Folding, and
Decorating to Create Books and More

BEVERLY MASSACHUSETTS

QUARRY BOOKS

Heather Weston

A QUARTO BOOK

First published in the United States of America by
Quarry Books, a member of
Quayside Publishing Group
100 Cummings Center
Suite 406-L
Beverly, Massachusetts 01915-6101
Telephone: (978) 282-9590
Fax: (978) 283-2742
www.quarrybooks.com

Library of Congress Cataloging-in-Publication Data
Weston, Heather.
Bookcraft: Techniques for Binding, Folding, and Decorating to
Create Books and More / Heather Weston.
p. cm.
"A Quarto book."
Includes bibliographical references and index.
ISBN 978-1-59253-455-5
1. Bookbinding. 2. Books. I. Title.
Z271.W457 2008
686.3--dc22
                                        2008016278

ISBN-13: 978-1-59253-455-5
ISBN-10: 1-59253-455-4

QUAR.BOBI

Conceived, designed, and produced by
Quarto Publishing plc
The Old Brewery
6 Blundell Street
London N7 9BH

Senior editor: Lindsay Kaubi
Copy editor: Claire Waite Brown
Art director: Caroline Guest
Managing art editor: Anna Plucinska
Designer: Jon Wainwright
Photographer: Martin Norris
Illustrator: John Woodcock
Creative director: Moira Clinch
Publisher: Paul Carslake

Color Separation by Sang Choy International Pte Ltd, Singapore
Printed in Singapore by Star Standard Industries (PTE) Ltd

10 9 8 7 6 5 4 3 2 1

Contents

Whether you are making a simple pamphlet-stitched notebook or a complex multi-layered carousel book, making books by hand can be a highly rewarding creative pursuit. Bookbinding with paper dates back nearly 2,000 years to the invention of paper itself, and has had a rich and influential history. With such a heritage, it is not surprising that many creative methods of bookmaking have been perfected and celebrated—indeed it is such a highly established art form that its current development is enormously diverse and experimental. Recent developments in computer and print technology have enabled anyone with access to a computer and some basic bookbinding skills to create their own storybooks, bound journals, and artists' books. The medium has truly come of age.

Bookcraft is written for a range of skill levels, from absolute beginner to those with a good deal of previous experience, who would like to learn some new, experimental bindings. The *Bindings* chapter introduces a broad range of binding techniques in the form of progressive projects, so that starting at the beginning and following the projects through will enable you to accumulate the skills and techniques needed to master the more complex projects later in the book. For those of you who already have some basic bookbinding skills, it is possible to dip in and out of projects at any stage of the book. In the *Page and cover* chapter, a range of techniques for altering the flat page are described, which enable you to consider content for your books and the potential of the page's surface. The final chapter, *The complete book* showcases some exquisite examples of books, bindings, and book art from around the world and is there simply to inspire and to demonstrate the many possibilities of this rewarding art form.

introduction

Materials

Many of the materials used in bookbinding can be sourced from mainstream craft and art stores. However, there are some materials that are only available though specialist bookbinding suppliers, and although it is sometimes possible to improvise, you are likely to need to locate a stockist. There are an increasing number of good online suppliers, and a list of these can be located in the resources section on page 124.

Paper and card

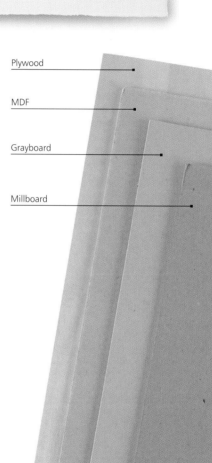

Plywood

MDF

Grayboard

Millboard

PAPER
There is an enormous range of paper available for the purposes of bookbinding, made in a variety of weights and sizes.

Weights and sizes
The main systems for measuring paper weight are pounds (lb) and grams per square meter (gsm), the former being used in the US and the latter in Europe and Asia. Conversion between the two can be complicated, so this book will translate between both systems of measurement.

Sizes of paper are also measured differently, and again there are two main systems: the International Standard (ISO), which uses A4 and its siblings; and the North American, which uses Letter, Legal, and Tabloid and their subsets. To close some of the ground between these two systems, measurements within this book are made in inches and in millimeters and centimeters, and the projects use a mixture of the common sizes.

Heavy or light?
Your paper choice is purely a matter of taste, but generally speaking it is preferable to use a lighter paper for small projects and a heavier paper for large ones, such as scrapbooks and drawing books.

Newsprint

Silicon release paper

Longevity

Most papers today are made by machine and have a relatively high acidity, and consequently degrade quite quickly. If you want a book to last years, or even generations, look for acid-free or archive-grade paper. Cheaper, poorer quality papers that do not need to stand the test of time are suitable for notebooks and short-life books.

Grain

The key feature of any sheet of paper is its grain. This is an important element to consider when bookbinding because it

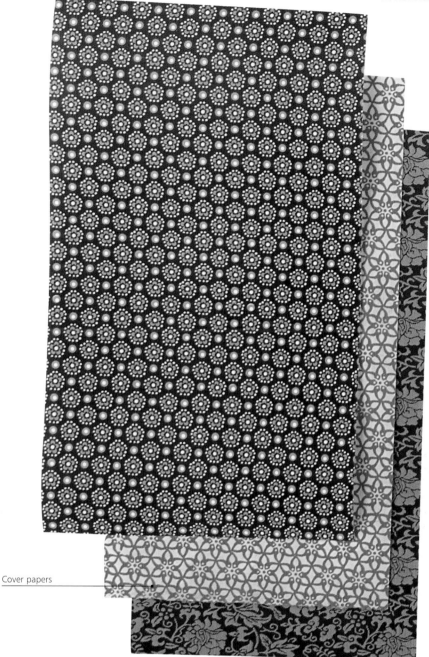

Cover papers

can dramatically affect results. This is discussed in more detail in the Rules section (see page 16).

Protective papers

Utility papers, such as newsprint, waxed paper, and absorbent scrap paper, are used constantly in bookbinding for a variety of purposes, including protecting your work surface, providing a base to glue out on, and protection of pages during the drying process. Kitchen paper is also an extremely useful material to help keep your hands free from dirt and glue.

BOARDS

Boards make up the stiff covers of hardback books and folios. There are different types of boards to choose from, each with their own advantages and disadvantages.

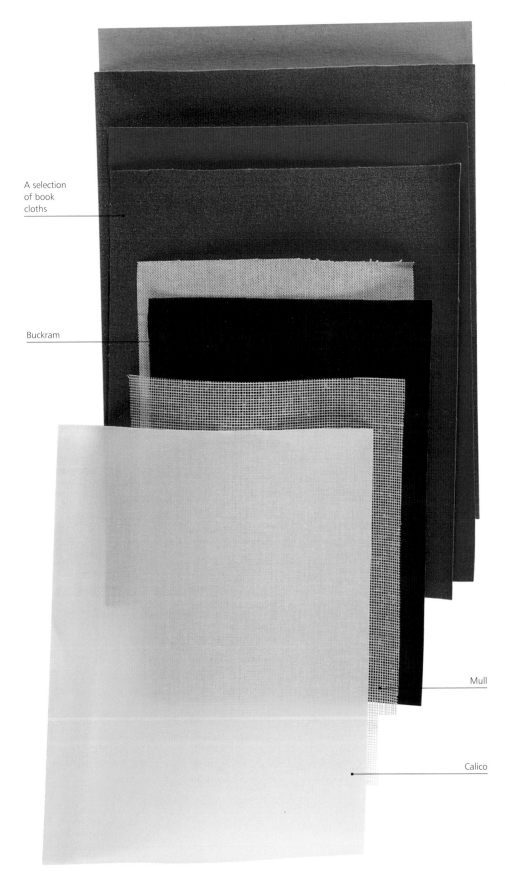

A selection of book cloths

Buckram

Mull

Calico

As a high-density fiberboard, millboard is considered to be the strongest and highest quality board. However, it is difficult to cut by hand and usually more expensive than the alternatives. Grayboard is less dense and lacks the strength of millboard, but is far easier to cut and cheaper to buy. Both come in a range of thicknesses, from $\frac{1}{16}$ in. (1.5 mm) to $\frac{1}{8}$ in. (3 mm).

Plywood, hardboard, and MDF can be used in place of board, but are more suitable for larger projects.

BOOK CLOTH AND COVER PAPERS

Book cloth was originally designed as a cheap, cotton-based alternative to leather, and has since become extremely popular as a cover material. It can be used to cover the whole book or in combination with other materials such as cover papers.

Book cloth and buckram are cotton-based sheet materials and are sold by length from the roll. Book cloth is lined with a fine paper layer that helps keep the material from misshaping and the glue from penetrating the cloth. There are a large number of book cloths available in different colors and finishes, although they are generally limited to specialist bookbinding suppliers. Buckram has a waterproof finish so can be wiped down.

Cover papers are an alternative to the cotton-based materials and provide a more decorative finish to a book. Many papers are manufactured or handmade specifically for the purpose, but it is also possible to use non-specific papers such as wrapping paper to cover your books. Cover papers are thinner and more malleable than book cloth and so tend to be much easier to apply.

MULL AND CALICO

Mull is an open-weave cream-colored muslin that is used in areas such as the spine, to strengthen adhesion between materials and stabilize glued areas. It is used in small amounts and is hidden from view once the book is complete. Calico is used for a similar purpose but has a closer weave and is white or gray in color.

GLUE

It is possible to do most bookmaking with a small range of glues. All the glues discussed here are water-soluble, so brushes should be washed with water and a little soap.

The use of glue is discussed in more detail in the Rules section (see page 17).

PVA glue

PVA (polyvinyl acetate) is an excellent adhesive and can be used widely in bookbinding. It is waterproof when dry and has a certain amount of elasticity and flexibility. It can also be watered down to make it less sticky to use. Be aware that PVA is quick-drying, so does not allow much correction time for repositioning.

Paste

Paste is a starch-based adhesive that is excellent for binding, and can be bought commercially or made at home from rice, corn, or wheat flour combined with water. It is generally slow-drying, so allows a little time for correcting wrongly positioned materials.

PVA/paste mix

A mixture of PVA and paste combines the slow-drying properties of paste and the faster-drying elastic properties of PVA. It is very easy to use and also allows for some correction time before drying.

Glue stick

A glue stick is useful for gluing small paper-to-paper areas, and has the advantage of being relatively moisture-free, preventing the paper from buckling during application.

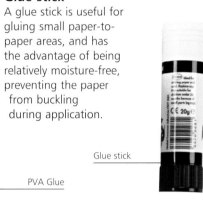

PVA Glue

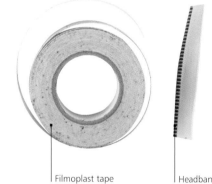

Glue stick

Filmoplast tape

Headband

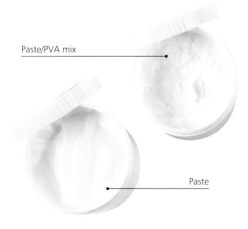

Paste/PVA mix

Paste

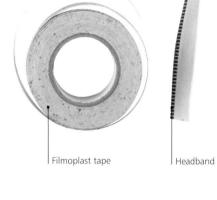

Bookmark ribbons

Linen tape

Polyester upholstery thread

Polyester upholstery thread

Cotton upholstery thread

Linen thread

THREADS

The thread you use for bookbinding must be strong enough to withstand movement within the book, but not so thick that it bulks up the spine too much. Some linen threads are made specifically for bookbinding. These are strong and come in a range of thicknesses (a good general-purpose one being 25/2), but where they are not available there are plenty of alternatives. Strong cotton or polyester upholstery thread can be used, and if you want to introduce a little color to your binding, there are a number to choose from.

Threads are sometimes waxed for use in bookbinding, to protect the thread and make it easier to use. You can wax your own thread by drawing it through a beeswax block, available from bookbinding suppliers.

OTHER MATERIALS

When making handmade books you will occasionally need other decorative or structural materials, such as headbands, adhesive or Filmoplast tapes, bookmark ribbons, binding screws, and linen tapes.

These are available from specialist suppliers and their uses are described in specific projects throughout the book.

Tools

There is a vast array of bookbinding tools available, but not all of them are essential kit. As with materials, many items are available from craft and art stores, but some can only be bought from specialist bookbinding suppliers. Certain tools can be expensive, so start off with the bare essentials before expanding your collection.

A selection of brushes

BRUSHES
Round-headed brushes are the most suitable for bookbinding projects. You will need at least one, but ideally a selection of three in different sizes. During longer projects it is useful to be able to change brushes halfway through to prevent clogging the brush with dried glue.

It is definitely beneficial to choose higher quality brushes, because cheap ones tend to lose bristles easily during gluing. An ideal size is between ½ and 1 in. (1.2 and 2.5 cm).

NEEDLES
While it is possible to do most projects with just one needle, it is useful to have a range at your disposal. Ideally the needle should be relatively small in size with a very sharp point and an eye of a size that will accommodate a range of threads.

A selection of awls

AWLS
Awls are used for making sewing holes in the spines of books and are available from craft stores and bookbinding suppliers. It is also possible to make your own awl using a short length—4 in. (10 cm)—of dowel into which a large, sharp-pointed needle is glued via a small, drilled hole.

You will occasionally need a hammer to help you punch your awl through thicker stacks of paper.

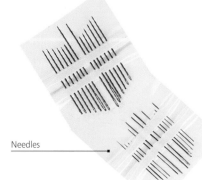

Needles

Bone folders

Teflon folder

BONE AND TEFLON FOLDERS

Bone folders are invaluable tools for creasing paper, but are also useful when making cloth or paper-bound book covers and for "sculpting" text or patterns into covers. Teflon folders are now available for those who prefer not to use bone. Most jobs can be done with one pointed-end bone or Teflon folder.

CUTTING EQUIPMENT

A large, self-healing cutting mat is an essential piece of equipment. This provides an excellent, long-lasting surface on which to cut board and paper.

A scalpel or similar is best for cutting paper and card, but a stronger craft knife is required for cutting board. Keep the blades sharp and clean by replacing them regularly. A pair of sharp scissors is useful for trimming threads and corners of book cloth.

Cutting mat

Scalpel

Craft knife

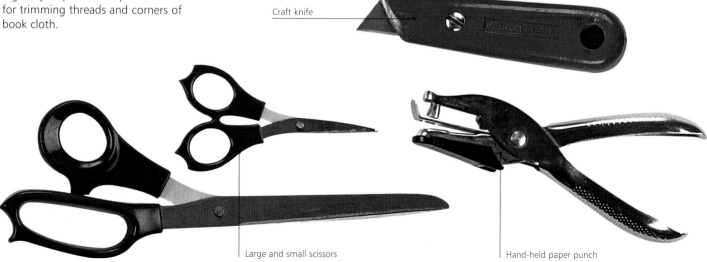

Large and small scissors

Hand-held paper punch

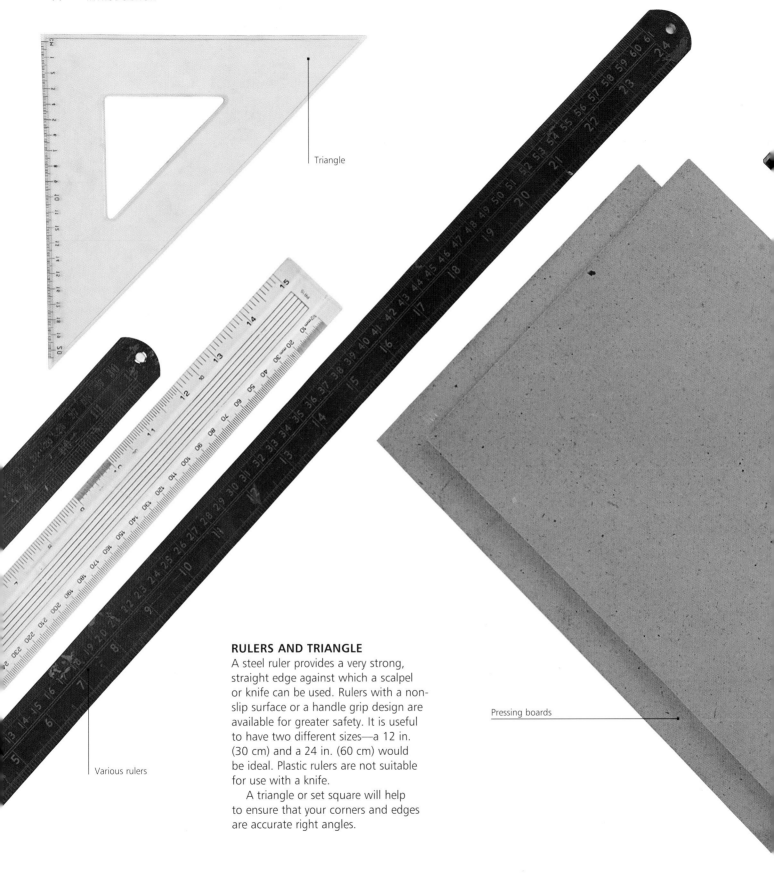

Triangle

Various rulers

Pressing boards

RULERS AND TRIANGLE

A steel ruler provides a very strong, straight edge against which a scalpel or knife can be used. Rulers with a non-slip surface or a handle grip design are available for greater safety. It is useful to have two different sizes—a 12 in. (30 cm) and a 24 in. (60 cm) would be ideal. Plastic rulers are not suitable for use with a knife.

A triangle or set square will help to ensure that your corners and edges are accurate right angles.

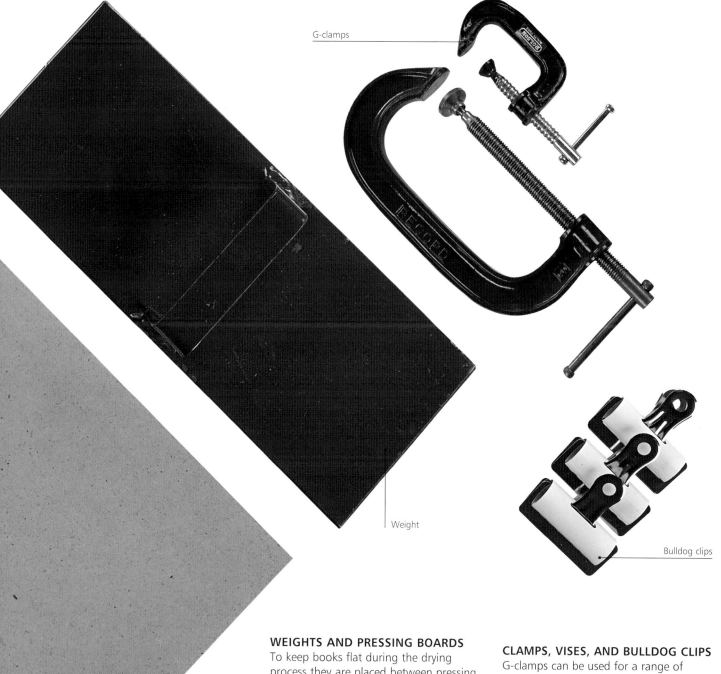

G-clamps

Weight

Bulldog clips

WEIGHTS AND PRESSING BOARDS

To keep books flat during the drying process they are placed between pressing boards with a weight on the top. This system can be improvised with a pile of books or offcuts from timber merchants and some heavy food cans. However, proper pressing boards are preferable because they are made from extremely dense fiberboard and so do not warp during the drying process. An alternative is plastic-coated plywood. Heavy weights can be found in junk stores but are also available from bookbinding suppliers.

CLAMPS, VISES, AND BULLDOG CLIPS

G-clamps can be used for a range of jobs, including pressing books flat (with pressing boards), applying pressure during debossing, and holding pages together during gluing and multi-section sewing. You will need two medium-sized clamps for these purposes. A vise, if you have access to one, is ideal for some gluing and sewing processes, although it is not an essential piece of kit.

Large bulldog clips are also very useful for gripping and clamping books during gluing, sewing, and drying.

Rules

There are a small number of fundamental rules that you should understand before embarking on bookmaking projects. Following these rules will improve your end results and ensure that the process of making is safe, consistent, and of a high quality.

GRAIN

The "grain" refers to the parallel structure of fibers that make up any paper or board. These run in one direction within the sheet, making it easier to bend and crease the paper *with* the grain rather than *against* it. When buying paper in sheets, the grain usually runs parallel to the long side of the sheet—although not always.

When making books, your end results will be superior if you ensure that the grain of your papers and boards runs in the same direction, usually from the head to the foot of the book. Any mixing of grain direction may cause the book to buckle and warp during drying.

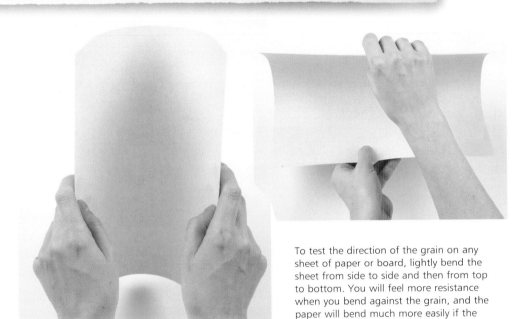

To test the direction of the grain on any sheet of paper or board, lightly bend the sheet from side to side and then from top to bottom. You will feel more resistance when you bend against the grain, and the paper will bend much more easily if the bend is parallel to the grain.

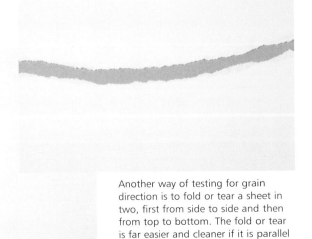

Another way of testing for grain direction is to fold or tear a sheet in two, first from side to side and then from top to bottom. The fold or tear is far easier and cleaner if it is parallel to the grain.

NOTE:

You need to know the direction of the grain before you start working with your materials, so it is worth familiarizing yourself with the feel of the grain in various types of paper—it can take some time to confidently assess grain direction.

CUTTING PAPER AND BOARD

When cutting raw materials such as paper, card, and board, it is vital that you protect your work surface from damage by using a cutting mat. This also provides a flat, smooth surface on which to cut clean lines.

Using a scalpel and steel ruler on a cutting mat achieves the best and safest results in the absence of a guillotine. Draw the blade toward you using several light strokes rather than a few heavy ones. When holding the steel ruler, keep your fingers well away from the cutting edge so that any slips of the blade will not result in cut fingers.

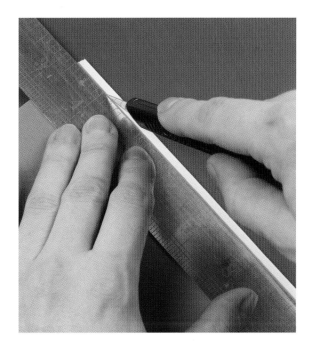

NOTES:

• Always keep your blades sharp and clean.

• Finger thimbles can be worn for protection if necessary. A non-slip backing on your steel ruler will also help protect your digits.

GLUING

Gluing may seem a simple part of bookmaking, but there are several useful rules to follow when gluing out materials for your books. First of all, make sure your work surface is covered with scrap paper or newsprint. Second, use a brush that is the right size for the job: a small brush for a small area and a large brush for a large area.

Always begin gluing from the center of the sheet and work out toward the edges. This will prevent the sheet from moving under your brush and the brush from slipping under the sheet. You will need to adjust the positioning of your support hand while you work the full sheet. Always ensure that the full sheet is covered, right up to the edges, and work quickly to prevent the glue from drying before you have finished.

NOTE:

If you do end up with glue marks, the only way to remove them is to moisten the whole area—for example the whole front cover—and gently rub the mark away. If you simply moisten the area affected, you will end up with an unsightly moisture stain just in that area.

This chapter explores different ways of creating handmade books. Whether you are beginning with blank sheets in order to make your own sketchbook or journal, creating an heirloom from existing written pages, or making a book form for purely decorative enjoyment, there is a binding method to suit your purpose. Using and combining adhesive and non-adhesive methods, it is possible to create an enormous range of binding styles, from the very simple pamphlet stitch, involving a single piece of thread, to the complex carousel book, which combines stitching, gluing, cutting, folding, and binding. In each case the starting point is the paper, the nature of which is explored and exploited.

By working your way through this chapter you will accumulate a range of skills and techniques that can, once mastered, be applied, adapted, and transformed into an infinite range of end products based on your own ideas and borrowing techniques from any of the projects. Each of the sections is also self-contained, enabling you to dip in and out at various levels, and allowing you to acquire a different set of skills at each point.

CHAPTER ONE: bindings

Pamphlet-stitch binding

Using pamphlet stitch is the most basic way of binding a group
of sheets together with a hand-sewn stitch, and this stitch can
be used when making a wide range of small to medium pamphlets
or notebooks.

Pamphlet stitch is a non-adhesive binding that is one of the central building blocks of bookbinding. This simple stitch enables you to make an enormous variety of notebooks without having to master the intricacies of complex bindings. It is the perfect binding method for making your own blank notebooks, or you can use it as a way of binding together pre-prepared printed sheets.

Depending on the size of the book you want to make, you can use a three-, five-, or seven-hole stitch; the extra stitches providing added strength for a larger spine.

As you will see in the following two projects, the pamphlet-stitched notebook also forms the basis of the single- and multi-section case-bound books.

DEFINING CHARACTERISTICS
The basic pamphlet stitch is a three-point stitching method that you can use to bind a batch of pages folded at their centers. An outer sheet of heavier paper or card is usually used as a cover to help protect the inner pages—all are bound into the stitch. For best results you should use no more than fifteen sheets, otherwise the central fold of the book becomes too bulky to lie flat.

The thread that you choose should be strong and able to withstand and resist movement within the pages as the book is used. The stitch is tied off with a reef knot to secure the thread ends and fix the pages in place. The advantage of this kind of binding is its simplicity and breadth of application. It is, however, limited by the number of sheets it will accommodate and the size of booklet this simple binding can hold securely.

Construction of a pamphlet-stitch binding

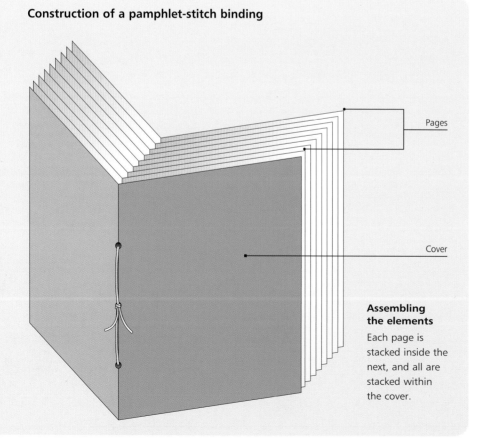

Pages

Cover

Assembling the elements

Each page is stacked inside the next, and all are stacked within the cover.

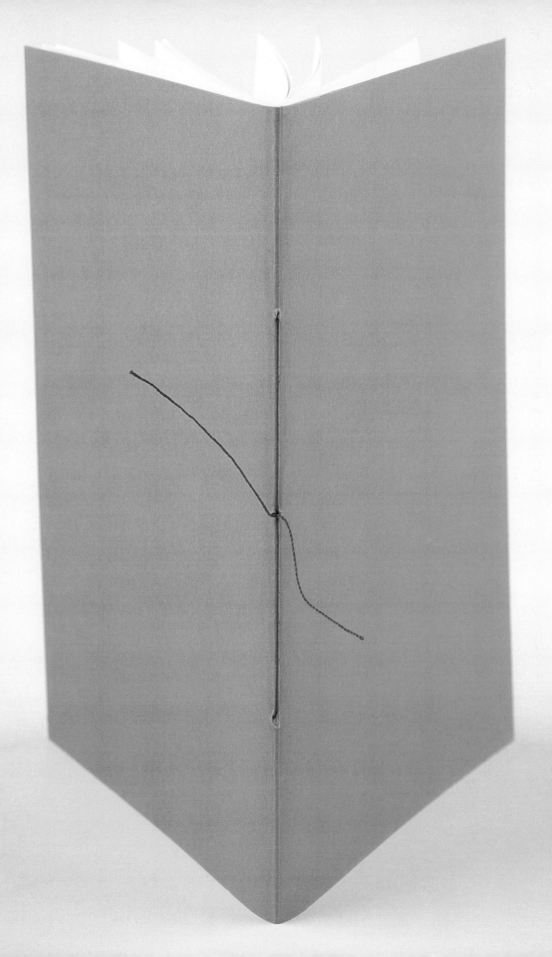

Materials

- **Book block:** ten sheets 70 lb (100 gsm) paper, approximately 6 x 8 in. (15 x 20 cm)
- **Cover:** one sheet 120 lb (270 gsm) card, approximately 6 x 8 in. (15 x 20 cm), with grain parallel to the short edge
- **Strong thread**

Tools

- Bone folder
- Pencil
- Awl
- Scissors
- Needle
- Scalpel, steel ruler, and cutting mat

CREATING A PAMPHLET-STITCH NOTEBOOK

Step 1
Fold each sheet of paper and the sheet of card in half and use a bone folder to ensure that the fold line is sharp and flat. Arrange the sheets one inside the next and put the cover sheet on the outside. Knock the base of the book to ensure all sheets are flush with each other.

Step 2
Use a pencil to mark three stitch holes along the inside fold, starting at the center and equally dividing the spine along its length. Pierce the holes from the inside to the outside using an awl.

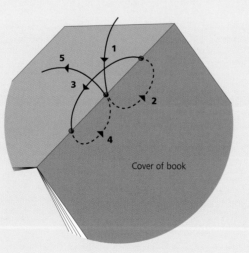

Three-hole stitch order
Starting from the outside of the book, follow the numerical order of stitches. Dotted lines show the stitches on the underside of the work.

Cover of book

Step 3
Cut a length of strong thread about three times the length of your spine and thread it onto your needle. Starting on the outside, draw your thread through the center hole, leaving a tail of about 4 in. (10 cm) on the end of the thread. Follow the order of stitching shown in the diagram, left. The final stitch should be through the center hole.

Step 4

Ensure that both ends of thread are either side of the central thread. Tug the threads taut and tie a reef knot over the central thread (see diagram below). Trim the threads to within 1 in. (2.5 cm) of the knot.

VARIATIONS

Once you have mastered the basic method of pamphlet-stitch binding, the process can be varied in a number of ways.

- If you want your stitching to be less visible, try beginning the sewing from the inside and tying off the knot within the center pages of the book.
- Add a contrasting endpaper to increase visual or functional effect.
- With larger books, use a five- or seven-stitch variation (see pages 24–29).

Reef knot

Take one thread in each hand. Pass the right thread over the left thread and under the loop. Now pass the left thread over the right thread and under the loop. Pull taut at each stage.

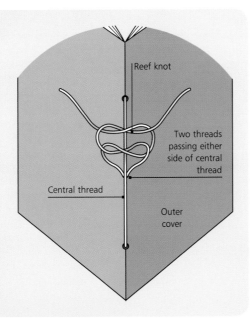

Reef knot

Two threads passing either side of central thread

Central thread

Outer cover

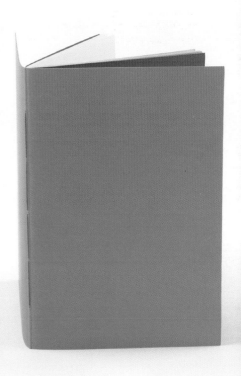

Step 5

Use a scalpel and steel ruler to trim the fore-edge (long, open edge) of the book with a scalpel. You may be able to do this by eye, but otherwise measure from the spine and mark where you need to cut. You will need to use several cuts of the scalpel to trim through the whole book. Finally, check that the top of the book is also neat and even—if it is ragged, trim it in the same way as the fore-edge.

Single-section case-binding

Probably one of the most versatile and ubiquitous of bindings, the single-section case binding is suitable for creating an enormous range of books, from large scrapbooks and sketchbooks to small pocket notebooks.

The basic principles of this binding method remain the same across its various applications and are relatively simple to master. Its versatility comes from the different ways in which its various ingredients can be modified in size, shape, color, and treatment.

The hardback "case" is made separately from the stitched book block, and the two parts are brought together in the final "casing-in" process.

If a large letter-size sketchbook or scrapbook is being created, then the weight/thickness of the grayboard that constitutes the "hardback" will need to be heavier/thicker, and the number of stitches used to stitch the book block will need to increase. For small books, three stitch-holes will be sufficient, but for a larger book this may need to increase to five or seven stitches to achieve stability within the binding. The book cloth that is used to cover the grayboard comes in a huge variety of colors and styles, including cotton, silk, and buckram. If appropriate, it is also possible to use a heavy paper in place of book cloth, to achieve similar results.

DEFINING CHARACTERISTICS
What defines this binding is its hard, protective cover, made from compact board (grayboard) covered with book cloth or paper. The "single-section" refers to the single batch of "spreads" that are stitched together in the center with thread. The basis is the pamphlet-stitched book block (see pages 20–23), but in order for it to be bound within a hard cover, a piece of mull is added to strengthen the adhesion between the book block and the case. The advantage of this kind of binding is that it will lie relatively flat when opened fully, without cracking or breaking the spine. This binding is only limited by the number of sheets that can be accommodated within it—usually no more than about 15, depending on size and thickness.

Construction of a single-section case-binding

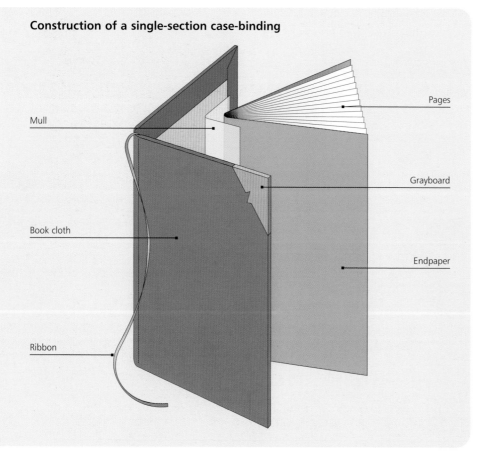

Mull

Book cloth

Ribbon

Pages

Grayboard

Endpaper

Materials

- **Book block:** ten sheets 85 lb (160 gsm) paper, 6 x 8 in. (15 x 20 cm)
- **Endpaper:** two sheets 85 lb (160 gsm) paper, 6 x 8 in. (15 x 20 cm)
- **Mull strip:** 5½ x 2 in. (14 x 5 cm)
- **Strong thread**
- **Scrap paper**
- **Book cloth:** 8¼ x 11 in. (21 x 28 cm)
- **Grayboard:** two sheets ¹⁄₁₆ in. (1.5 mm) thick, 6¼ x 4 in. (16 x 10.5 cm)
- **PVA/paste mix**
- **Ribbon:** ⅛ in. (3 mm) wide, 8 in. (20 cm) long

Tools

- Bone folder
- Pencil
- Awl
- Scissors
- Needle
- Scalpel, steel ruler, and cutting mat
- Glue brush
- Cloth
- Book weight or heavy, flat object
- Two pressing boards

PREPARING THE BOOK BLOCK

Step 1
Assemble your book block following the instructions for Creating a pamphlet-stitch notebook (see Step 1, page 22), using a 90 lb (180 gsm) endpaper in place of the card cover.

Step 2
Make a crease in the mull strip by folding it in half lengthwise. Open up the strip and position it on the outside of the book, with the crease over the spine. This will aid adhesion between the book block and the case.

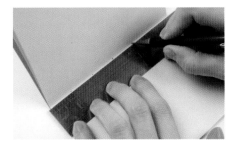

Step 3
Beginning at the center, mark five points at equal intervals along the inner spine. With an awl, pierce the five holes all the way through.

Step 4
Take a length of thread about three times the length of the spine, and begin the five-stitch sewing at the center hole, from the outside. Follow the order of stitching shown in the diagram, leaving a 4 in. (10 cm) tail to enable you to tie off easily later. Once all the holes have been sewn, pull the thread tight, making sure that they are at either side of the center stitch. Tie a reef knot (see page 23). Use a scalpel and steel ruler to trim the top, bottom, and fore-edge of the pages.

NOTES:

- Take care not to pierce the thread as you stitch through the holes, because this will prevent you from being able to tie the thread tightly.

- Wherever you begin the sewing is where the final knot will be tied. You may decide you would like the knot on the inside in the center of the book. If so, start from the inside.

Measurements of elements
These measurements remain more or less constant irrespective of the size of your book.

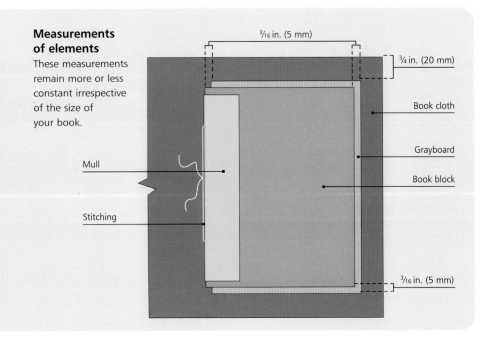

3/16 in. (5 mm)
3/4 in. (20 mm)
Book cloth
Grayboard
Book block
Mull
Stitching
3/16 in. (5 mm)

Five-hole stitch order
Starting from the outside of the book and at the center hole, follow the numerical order of stitching. The dotted lines show the underside of the stitches.

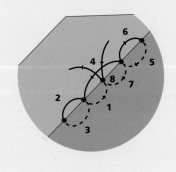

PREPARING THE CASE

Step 1
With a large piece of scrap paper under your work, glue all over the back of the book cloth, working from the center toward the edges. Leaving enough space for the spine (see panel), place the two pieces of grayboard on the glued cloth, making sure the tops and bottoms are straight and level. Press the boards firmly in place.

Step 2
Diagonally cut off each corner of the book cloth within about ³⁄₁₆ in. (5 mm) of the corner of the board. Using a steel ruler, carefully fold the long edges of the book cloth over onto the board, ensuring that the cloth is evenly pressed down.

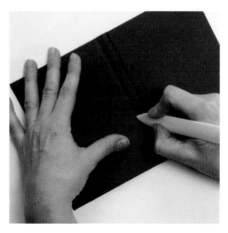

Step 3
Using a bone folder, tuck in the cloth around each corner, where cloth meets board. Once this is done, fold over the short edges and ensure that they are smoothly pressed down. It may be necessary to reapply glue, especially on the areas of tucked-in cloth.

Step 4
Run a bone folder along the outside of the spine to define the spine edges more clearly. Place the case under a flat, clean weight while it dries.

MEASURING THE SPINE GAP

1 The spine gap will vary from book to book depending on the thickness of the book block.

2 To measure the spine gap, place the boards at the front and back of your book block. Boards should protrude about ³⁄₁₆ in. (5 mm) at top, bottom, and fore-edge. The spine should overhang the boards by about ³⁄₁₆ in. (5 mm) along the spine edge.

3 With a small strip of paper, mark the distance from the spine edge of the front cover to the spine edge of the back cover, around the spine. This is how big your spine gap should be.

4 When placing the boards on the glued cloth, use a strip of card the width of the measured spine to ensure that the boards are the right distance apart. This strip is just for measuring and should not be glued in.

Using a strip of paper, measure the width of the spine from the front cover to the back cover.

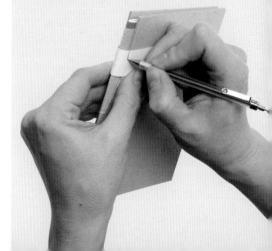

CASING-IN

Casing-in is the final process of attaching the book block to the case. It creates a strong, adhesive binding that can withstand rough handling.

Step 1

If you would like your book to have a ribbon page-holder, now is the time to attach it. Take a length of ⅛ in. (3 mm) ribbon, approximately one-and-a-half times the height of your case's spine, and glue it in position as shown.

Step 2

Take your book block and place a sheet of scrap paper between the front cover and first page—it should be significantly larger than the book block in order to protect the rest of it while you are gluing. Glue out the front cover of the book block, starting from the center and moving outward to the edges, including gluing over the area of mull.

Step 3

Once the front cover is glued, carefully remove the scrap paper and, with both hands, position the glued front cover onto the front inside of the case. Ensure that it is placed with an even amount of cover edge showing at top, side, and bottom. Smooth the cover down in position with a dry, clean cloth or your fingers.

> **NOTE:**
>
> Make sure you do not get glue anywhere other than on the cover, because this could result in the pages becoming stuck together.

Step 4

Glue out the book block's back cover in exactly the same way, not forgetting to use the scrap paper between the cover sheet and first page. Position the cover onto the inside back cover of the case, again checking that it is evenly positioned. You will need to lift the front cover at 90 degrees to allow the glued back page to reach the back cover properly. Smooth down the glued area as before.

Step 5

Once the book block is attached to the case, place a clean sheet of scrap paper between the case and the first page, at both back and front. This will help absorb the excess moisture from the glue as it dries and prevent the pages of your book from buckling. Place your book flat under pressing boards and a heavy weight to dry.

VARIATION

Try making a large case-bound sketchbook using the same principles.

1 Use larger sheets of paper, endpaper, grayboard, and book cloth as follows:

2 **Book block:** ten sheets good-quality cartridge/drawing paper, 90 lb (175 gsm), 8½ x 11 in. (21.5 x 28 cm)

3 **Endpapers:** two sheets 100 lb (220 gsm) paper, same size as the pages

4 **Grayboard:** two sheets 8½ x 11¼ in. (21.5 x 28.5 cm)

5 **Book cloth:** 13¼ x 20½ in. (33.5 x 49 cm)

6 Follow the instructions as before and apply the same principles of assembly.

7 This uses a slightly thicker grade of grayboard, which will help the covers to remain flat and strong.

8 Try using a seven-hole pamphlet stitch when sewing the book block to strengthen the bind when making large books.

Seven-hole stitch order

Starting from the outside of the book and at the center hole, follow the numerical order. The dotted lines show the underside of the stitches.

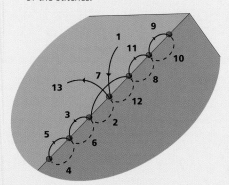

Multi-section case-binding

The multi-section binding is the king of binding structures and is one of the most recognizable. Its sewn and glued structure is strong and durable, making it suitable for binding an important book that needs to stand the test of time.

The multi-section case-bound book is the most traditional book format, dating back nearly 2,000 years. This system of sewn, folded sheets replaced the scroll and quickly became extremely popular due to its ease of handling, portability, and potential to store enormous amounts of information. Its structure also meant that both sides of the sheet could be written on, and the pages accessed at any and all points, quickly and easily.

This form of book was very important in the development of Christianity, because it allowed the scriptures to be taken far and wide. The modern incarnation of this format is the hardback book. Take a close look at almost any dictionary, encyclopedia, or first edition and the multi-section structure is visible. This method is recognized by binders as the best and strongest way of binding pages together, its only limitation being the cost of production.

There are a number of ways to achieve a multi-section binding, but here you will learn a simplified version of the hardback book made of four sections (64 pages) sewn into a quarter-bound hard cover.

DEFINING CHARACTERISTICS

The multi-section book can be thought of as several single-section books—like the pamphlet-stitch book on pages 20–23—stitched together using a special stitch and strengthened with the addition of linen tape at intervals down the spine. Take a closer look at a multi-section hardback book, and you will notice sometimes as many as twenty sections sewn together to form the book block. These are then case-bound into a hard cloth- or buckram-covered board-based case, with endpapers used to attach the book block to the case. Most large multi-section books have a rounded spine and many have their title foiled onto their spine or cover.

This binding is characteristically strong and durable and is therefore ideal for material that is subject to heavy use over a long period of time. It also has the advantage of lying flat when opened, so is also a suitable binding for sturdy notebooks and sketchbooks.

Construction of a multi-section case binding

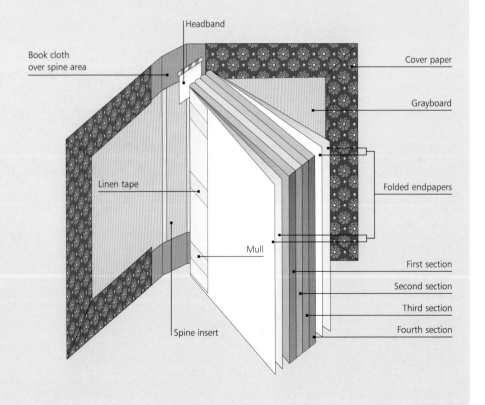

Headband

Book cloth over spine area

Cover paper

Grayboard

Linen tape

Folded endpapers

Mull

First section

Second section

Third section

Fourth section

Spine insert

Materials

- **Book block:** 32 sheets 70 lb (100 gsm) paper, 8½ x 11 in. (21.5 x 28 cm)—choose four different colors, eight sheets of each.
- **Endpapers:** two sheets 80 lb (150 gsm) paper, 8½ x 11 in. (21.5 x 28 cm)
- **Strong thread**
- **Linen tape:** three strips 3 x ⅜ in. (8 x 1 cm)
- **Masking tape**
- **PVA/paste mix**
- **Scrap paper**
- **Waxed paper**
- **PVA glue**
- **Mull strip:** 8 x 2½ in. (20 x 6.5 cm)
- **Headband:** ½ in. (12 mm) strip
- **Card strip for spine insert:** 120 lb (270 gsm) card
- **Grayboard:** two sheets, ⅛ in. (2 mm) thick, the same width as your book block and ¼ in. (6 mm) taller
- **Book cloth:** one piece 3 in. (7.5 cm) wide and 2 in. (5 cm) taller than the grayboard
- **Cover paper:** two sheets, the same width as your grayboard and 1 in. (2.5 cm) taller at the top and bottom

Tools

- Bone folder
- Pencil
- Awl
- Scissors
- Needle
- Table or block of wood
- Glue brush
- Book weight or heavy, flat object
- Scalpel, steel ruler, and cutting mat
- Heavy-duty guillotine (optional)

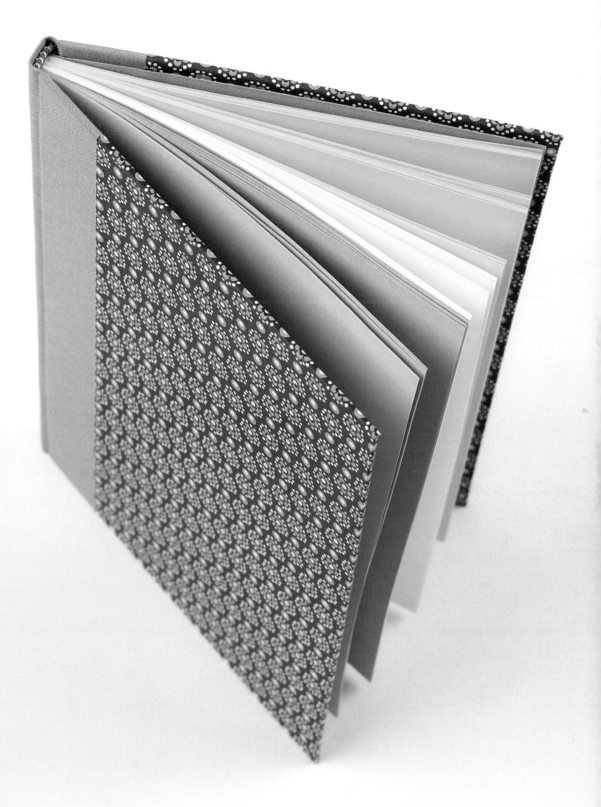

MAKING THE BOOK BLOCK

First you need to make the multi-section book block that will constitute the pages of your book. Here, the simplest sewing method is used where the stitches run parallel to the spine, this is suitable for books with a small number of sections.

Step 1

Accurately fold each of your sheets, including the endpapers, using a bone folder to sharpen each fold as you go. Then assemble your sheets into four sections of eight sheets, each placed inside each other. You should end up with four stacked sections and two separate folded endpapers.

Step 2

The spines of each section need to be marked for stitch holes—for this multi-section binding you will require eight stitches per section. With a pencil, mark the stitch holes (alternatively known as sewing stations) at the following points along the inside fold of each stack: ½, 2, 2½, 4, 4½, 6, 6½, and 8 in. (1.5, 5, 6.5, 10, 11.5, 15, 16.5, and 20 cm). Pierce each hole with an awl from the inside to the outside of your sheets—each section can be done in one go.

Here a template was used for marking stitch holes. To do this yourself, simply take a sheet of scrap paper the same size as your pages and mark the stitch points along the edge of the sheet. This ensures greater consistency when marking each section.

Eight-hole stitch order

Sections 1 and 3 are sewn from tail to head, whereas sections 2 and 4 are sewn from head to tail. The dotted lines show the underside of the stitch.

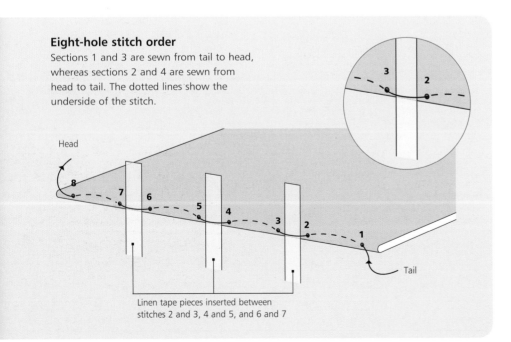

Head

Tail

Linen tape pieces inserted between stitches 2 and 3, 4 and 5, 6 and 7

Step 3

Cut a length of strong thread about six times the length of your spine and thread it onto your needle. Take your first section of book and, starting from the outside and at the tail end, draw the thread through the first hole, leaving about 4 in. (10 cm) of thread at the end. Follow the stitch order shown in the diagram until you get to the head of the section.

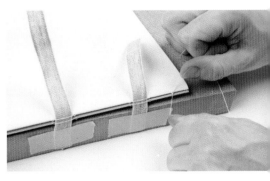

Step 4

Insert strips of linen tape under stitches 2 and 3, 4 and 5, and 6 and 7. These tapes will ultimately strengthen the bind. Pull the thread taut so that it grips the tapes (pull in the direction of the spine and remember to grip the other end of the thread, otherwise it will simply pull right through). Use masking tape to fix the ends of the linen tapes, with the book attached, to the edge of a table or block of wood, to help with stability while sewing.

Step 5

Take your second section of sheets and, lining them up with the first, thread the needle through the head hole at the top. Then follow the stitch order in the opposite direction, making sure you entrap the linen tape strips but being careful not to penetrate them with the needle. When you reach the tail of the book, tie a knot with the loose thread that was left at the tail of the first section—this will secure the two sections together. Ensure that this knot brings the sections together tightly.

Step 6

Take your third section of sheets and, aligning it with the holes of the other two, sew up in the opposite direction to the previous section. When you get to the head stitch hole you will need to secure this section to the previous one using a "kettle" stitch. This is a stitch that loops back around the previous head stitch that linked sections one and two. Once you have done this, pull the thread taut and begin attaching the fourth section, starting with the head stitch.

> **NOTE:**
>
> Between each stitching it is important to re-press the folds of the sections together with the bone folder, because the spine is liable to swell due to the folds and the stitching adding bulk. Keep the thread taut at all times.

NOTE:

If you are sewing more than four sections together, simply continue with Steps 5 and 6 until you get to your last section, and finish with Step 7. For larger stacks of sections it is not possible to do a final tie-off using the loose beginning stitch.

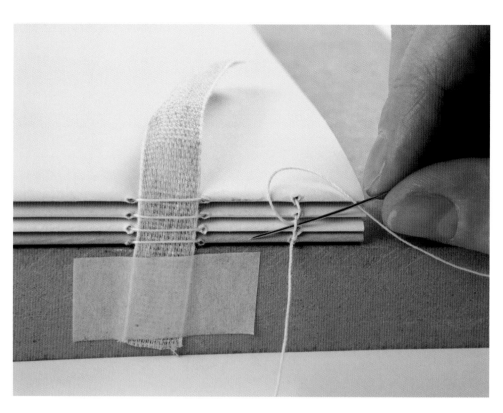

Step 7

Once you have reached the tail stitch of the fourth section, tie a double kettle stitch under the previous section's tail stitch, and pull taut. For extra security tie a reef knot (see page 23) with the loose thread from the beginning stitch.

Step 8

The simplest way to attach endpapers to the sewn book block is by "tipping in," or applying a ³⁄₁₆ in. (5 mm) strip of paste down one side of the spine edge of the endpaper and attaching it to one side of the sewn book block, under the linen tapes. To achieve this cleanly, mask off the rest of your endpaper with scrap paper and brush the exposed area with glue. Start from the center and work out to each end. Attach the glued endpaper at one end of the book so that spine, head, and tail line up with your book block. You can then do the same at the other end with the second endpaper. Dry under a flat, heavy weight.

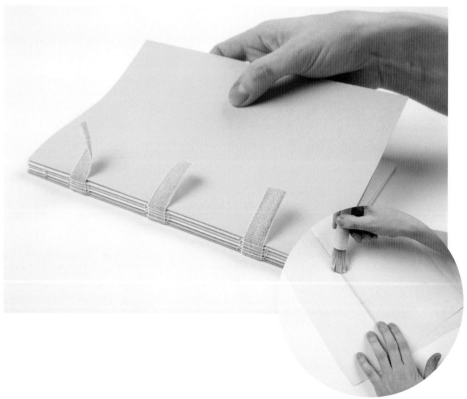

Step 9

Place the book block at the edge of a table or block of wood—with waxed paper underneath and on top to protect the table and weight from glue—so that the spine protrudes by about ½ in. (1.5 cm), and place a flat weight on top. Thoroughly coat the spine with PVA glue, ensuring that you glue the valleys between the sections. Leave to dry under the weight for twenty minutes. Add another layer of glue along the spine and carefully attach the strip of mull so that it overlaps each side of the spine by about 1 in. (2.5 cm). Press this firmly in place, ensuring that it is thoroughly embedded in the glue, adding more glue if necessary.

Tap head and tail so that they are flush and dry the book block under the weight, again with the addition of waxed paper to protect other surfaces.

Step 10

Use a scalpel and steel ruler to carefully trim about ⅛ in. (3 mm) from the head, tail, and fore-edge of your book block, so that they are smooth and square. Alternatively, with a thick book block you may prefer to use a heavy-duty guillotine. Trim the three linen tapes so that they are flush with the edge of the mull.

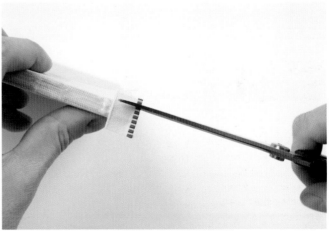

Step 11

To add a headband, apply PVA to the top ½ in. (12 mm) of the head of your spine, then attach the piece of headband so that the colored part protrudes above the book block. Trim the excess headband from the sides of the spine so that what remains protrudes about 1/16 in. (2 mm) at each side of the spine.

MAKING THE FLAT-BACK CASE

Casing-in your multi-section book block to a hard cover follows similar principles to that of the single-section binding project (see pages 28–29), but with slight amendments. Here you will case-in using the quarter-bound method, which uses book cloth on the spine but paper to cover the front and back covers. Exact measurements for materials are not given here, because final book blocks may differ in size slightly after trimming and depending on the thickness of your paper. Instead, follow the principles explained.

Step 1

Cut a strip of thick card as tall as your book and slightly wider than its spine—this will be your spine insert. Cut your grayboard so that it is the same width as your book block and ¼ in. (6 mm) taller. Measure your spine gap (see page 27) but with the cover boards and spine insert both in place. The measurement represents the gap you will leave between the two boards when you glue the book cloth onto the spine area.

Step 2

Cut the book cloth so that it is 1 in. (2.5 cm) bigger at the top and bottom than your grayboard, and about 3 in. (7.5 cm) wide. Mark a vertical center line and mark the spine gap straddling the center line equally. With scrap paper underneath, glue out your piece of book cloth, then move it across to a fresh piece of scrap paper. Place the front and back grayboards on the cloth, each in line with the outer marks. Position the spine insert right in the middle of the center line and flush with the grayboard at top and bottom—this will form the flat spine of your book. Turn the top and tail of the cloth over and smooth in place, then define the inner spine area with the bone folder. Dry flat under a heavy weight.

Step 3

Take your first piece of cover paper and glue out the back on scrap paper. With your outside cover facing upward, place the glued paper so that it overlaps your spine cloth by about ¹⁄₁₆ in. (1.5 mm) down the book's length. Diagonally cut the corners off your cover paper so that it is within ¼ in. (6 mm) of the corners of your boards. With the help of a steel ruler, turn over the fore-edge cover paper and smooth it down. Turn the corners over with your bone folder and press them firmly in place. Then turn over the top and bottom of your cover paper. Repeat for the other cover paper.

CASING-IN

It is now time to complete the final process
of attaching the book block to the case.

Step 1

With a sheet of scrap paper under
the front endpaper of your book
block, glue out the endpaper,
ensuring that the mull and tapes
are thoroughly brushed with glue,
including under the linen tapes.
Position the endpaper onto the case
so that the head, tail, and fore-edge
are about ⅛ in. (3 mm) in from the
edge of the cover. Ensure that the
spine will sit neatly positioned on
the center of the spine insert, then
smooth down firmly.

Step 2

Repeat for the back endpaper,
making sure that both covers are
in the same position before firming
down. Redefine the spine area with
your bone folder. Finally, leave to
dry under a weight, with the
addition of scrap paper between
the two endpaper leaves at back
and front and on the outside of the
book—this will help absorb excess
moisture while drying and prevent
the pages buckling.

Perfect binding

Perfect binding is a method of binding single sheets of paper together using adhesive and without the need for sewing, and can be used to make a variety of books and notepads.

In its simplest form, perfect binding is the method used to bind utilitarian, tear-off memo pads. In its more complex form it can be used to bind paperback-style books and brochures. Although it had its origins in the nineteenth century, this binding method has been appropriated by the printing industry for the binding of mass-produced paperbacks, due to improvements in the quality of glues and because it is an inexpensive method that can be mechanized for commercial application. It is particularly suitable for low-use books, because overuse can lead to spine-cracking and the loss of pages from the bind.

DEFINING CHARACTERISTICS

A method used to bind a batch of single, same-size sheets using glue as the binding material, perfect binding can be used for thin and thick books alike, but does not afford a strong binding.

This method is best suited to binding uncoated, non-brittle papers, such as copy paper, writing or bond paper, or any other similar, non-glossy, absorbent paper. This type of paper provides the most adhesion between sheets. The glue used must be strong and flexible after drying, so PVA is the best choice. Each and every sheet is attached to the spine with a small amount of glue, so each can be torn off cleanly without destroying the bind or the sheet, a function perfectly suited to memo pads and jotters.

Construction of a perfect binding

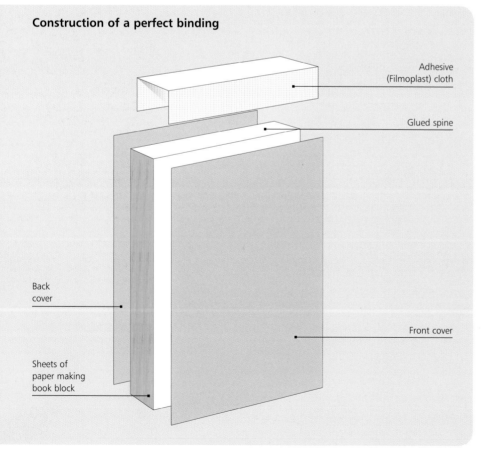

Adhesive (Filmoplast) cloth

Glued spine

Back cover

Front cover

Sheets of paper making book block

Materials

- ◆ Book block: 50 sheets 70 lb (100 gsm) paper, 8¼ x 5½ in. (21 x 14 cm)
- ◆ PVA glue
- ◆ Cover: two sheets 120 lb (270 gsm) card, 8¼ x 5½ in. (21 x 14 cm)
- ◆ Adhesive Filmoplast cloth: 5½ x 1 in. (14 x 2.5 cm), any color

Tools

- ◆ Guillotine
- ◆ Two pressing boards
- ◆ Vise or two G-clamps
- ◆ Two large bulldog clips (optional)
- ◆ Glue brush
- ◆ Pencil
- ◆ Scalpel, steel ruler, and cutting mat

BINDING THE BOOK BLOCK

To make this perfect-bound notepad, first a stack of papers is glued together at the spine.

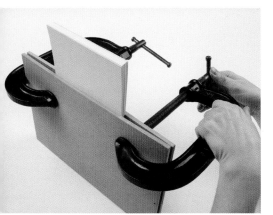

Step 1

Gather your sheets of paper together and ensure that they are flush at one of the short sides by tapping them firmly on the surface of your table—this flush edge will be your spine. If there are no flush sides, trim the sheets to the same size with a guillotine. Carefully place the gathered sheets between two pressing boards in a vise or using two G-clamps, keeping them flush. Allow half of the book to protrude above the boards.

Step 2

With one hand, push the whole of the spine to one side so that the pages are slightly splayed. With a brush and PVA, carefully glue the length of the spine while it is in this position. Remove your hand and let the spine return to its upright position. Then splay the spine in the other direction and glue again. Return to the upright position and leave to dry for ten minutes.

Step 3

Carefully loosen the book within the vise and adjust it so that it now only protrudes ¼ in. (6 mm) from the top of the boards—this will ensure that the spine will dry straight. Tighten the vise again and leave to dry for one hour or until the glue is dry and plastic.

"Double-fan" gluing method

Known as the "double-fan" method, here glue is not just pasted on the thin edge of each sheet but also very slightly down each side of the sheet. This helps one sheet to adhere to the next. Make sure the glue is confined to the spine area only.

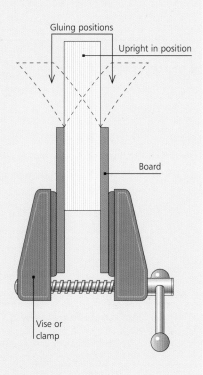

The book block is first pushed to the right, then glued, then pushed to the left, and glued again.

NOTE:

It is not easy to keep the pages flush as you are transferring them to the vise, so it may help to grip the pages with two bulldog clips along the spine while you do this.

ATTACHING THE COVER

The cover sheets are attached using adhesive cloth.

Step 1

Use a pencil to mark a faint line at the top of the front cover near where it will join the spine, about ⅜ in. (1 cm) down from the top.

Step 2

Place the two cover sheets at the front and back of your book and return it to the pressing boards, leaving about 1 in. (2.5 cm) protruding at the top. Make sure the spine and covers are level and absolutely flush.

Step 3

Position the length of adhesive Filmoplast cloth onto the front cover so that about ⅜ in. (1 cm) overlaps the cover itself. Ensure that this is level, then pull the tape over the spine and down onto the back cover. Ensure that it is a tight fit and smooth down with your thumb.

Step 4

Trim the sides and tail of the book with a guillotine, if necessary. Alternatively use a sharp scalpel.

Post binding

Post binding is a non-adhesive method of binding loose sheets of paper using two-piece binding screws, or posts, and can be used in very simple or more complex bindings.

In this project you will learn the very simple principles behind binding with posts, in softback and hardback form. These bindings can range from fan-like, single-post bindings, where all sheets can be made visible at once, to two- or three-post booklet bindings and more sophisticated case-bound versions, where the screws are hidden from view.

Post binding is the ideal choice for material that is subject to amendment and change, such as a menu or swatchbook, and can be achieved using a hand-held hole punch or a more heavy-duty paper drill, depending on the thickness of your material. Although this can be a strong method of binding, it is often used to bind more ephemeral books.

DEFINING CHARACTERISTICS

Binding with posts provides a non-permanent way of fixing pages together, allowing you the flexibility of opening up the binding to add or subtract sheets at a later date. As your book is added to, larger posts or post extensions can be substituted along the way.

In order to fit the binding screws a hole is first punched into your sheets of paper, either individually or as a stack.

The two-part screw is then fitted from either side of the hole and tightened in place. Binding screws are available in plastic, steel, nickel, aluminum, and brass, and are known by a variety of names including screw posts, push-lock screws (plastic), and binding posts. They range in size from about $\frac{1}{8}$ to 3 in. (3 to 75 mm), depending on the type. Screw extensions range from $\frac{1}{4}$ to 1 in. (6 to 25 mm).

Post binding does not allow for a book to be opened fully and flat, so you will gain a more comfortable and fuller opening if you use a landscape orientation.

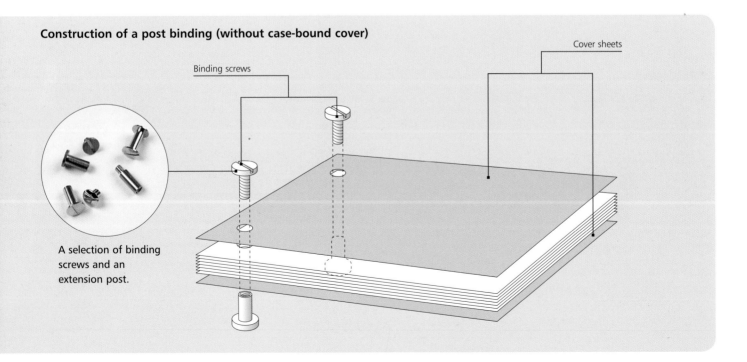

Construction of a post binding (without case-bound cover)

Binding screws

Cover sheets

A selection of binding screws and an extension post.

Materials

- **Book block:** 50 sheets 70 lb (100 gsm) paper, 8¼ x 5½ in. (21 x 14 cm)
- **Cover:** two sheets 120 lb (270 gsm) card, 8¼ x 5½ in. (21 x 14 cm)
- **Two nickel or brass binding screws:** ¼ in. (6 mm) capacity
- **Spare card:** 8¼ x 5½ in. (21 x 14 cm)

To make a case-bound version you will also need:
- **Book cloth:** two pieces, 12 x 8 in. (30 x 20 cm) two pieces 5¾ x 2 in. (14.5 x 5 cm)
- **Grayboard:** two sheets ¹⁄₁₆ in. (1.5 mm) thick, 8¾ x 6 in. (22 x 15 cm) two sheets ¹⁄₁₆ in. (1.5 mm) thick, 6 x 1 in. (15 x 2.5 cm)
- **Lining paper:** two sheets 8¼ x 5½ in (21 x 14 cm)
- **PVA/paste mix**
- **Two binding screws:** ½ in (12 mm) capacity

Tools

- Pencil
- Ruler
- Single-hole hand punch
- Two screwdrivers
- Scalpel, steel ruler, and cutting mat

To make a case-bound version you will also need:
- Bone folder
- Glue brush
- Book weight or heavy, flat object

MAKING A SIMPLE POST-BOUND BOOK

The following step-by-step sequence shows you how to make the simplest version of a post-bound book.

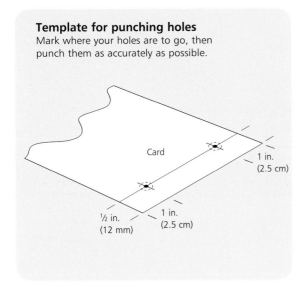

Template for punching holes
Mark where your holes are to go, then punch them as accurately as possible.

Card

1 in. (2.5 cm)

½ in. (12 mm)

1 in. (2.5 cm)

Step 1
The first step is to punch the holes in each sheet. When using a single-hole hand punch the easiest way to produce a consistent and accurate punch for each page is to use a sheet of card as a template. Take a spare sheet of card of the same dimensions as your page and mark on it where you would like the screws to sit—this is usually about ½ in. (12 mm) in from the spine edge and about 1 in. (2.5 cm) from the head and tail. Punch the holes in the template according to your marks.

Step 2
Position your template exactly over the sheet and punch through the holes in the guide. Repeat this for every sheet, including the cover sheets.

NOTE:

If you have access to a two-hole heavy-duty punch, or a single-hole paper drill, simply mark the top sheet and punch according to this—several sheets or even all of them may be punched at once.

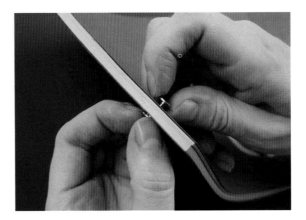

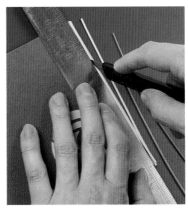

Step 3
Gather all the punched sheets together with covers at front and back. Take the long piece of the binding screw and put it through the punched hole from the bottom, then screw in the short piece from the top. Tighten with two screwdrivers, one holding the top screw in place, the other tightening the screw. Some binding screws have screwdriver slots in both constituent parts, whereas others have one smooth-topped part and one slotted part. Plastic binding screws often have a snap-shut mechanism.

Step 4
Use a scalpel and steel ruler to carefully trim the head, tail, and fore-edge, so that they are smooth and square.

MAKING COVERS FOR A POST-BOUND BOOK

This type of hinged cover will bind the book that you have just made, but allows you to conceal the screws within the spine.

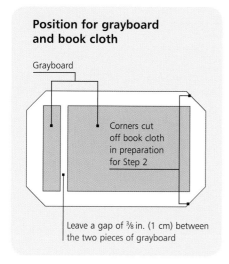

Position for grayboard and book cloth

Grayboard

Corners cut off book cloth in preparation for Step 2

Leave a gap of ³⁄₈ in. (1 cm) between the two pieces of grayboard

Step 1

Glue out one of the larger pieces of book cloth and position the grayboard—one small piece and one large piece—centrally on the cloth, leaving a ³⁄₈ in. (1 cm) hinge gap between the two pieces of board.

Step 2

Cut the corners of the book cloth and fold the short edges onto the grayboard. Smooth down, making sure the small piece of grayboard does not move out of position while doing so. Using a bone folder, tuck in the corners (see Step 3, page 27), then fold over the long edges using a steel ruler. Smooth these down firmly.

Step 3

Glue one of the small pieces of book cloth and attach this over the hinge area, as shown. Again, define the hinge area with your bone folder. This hinge will enable the book to open more fully. Leave the cover to dry under a flat weight.

Step 4

To finish each cover, glue out the two sheets of lining paper and position on the inside of each cover. Ensure that these are firmly and smoothly attached. Repeat Steps 1–4 for the second cover-board.

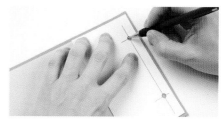

Step 5

Using your hole template again, mark the position of the holes for the binding posts in the small hinged area—the template should sit about ¹⁄₈ in. (3 mm) in from the edges of the cover. Punch right through the cloth and board of each cover.

Step 6

Position your book block, with the screws removed, so that the holes line up with the covers' holes as shown, and screw the wider binding posts in. Finally, flip both the covers over so that they are positioned over the pages.

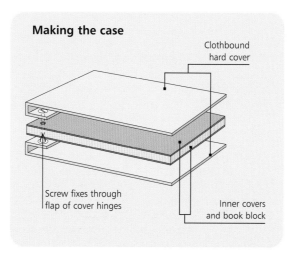

Making the case

Clothbound hard cover

Screw fixes through flap of cover hinges

Inner covers and book block

NOTE:

Without a paper drill you may need several goes at making the holes, and the aid of a scalpel to cut through the book cloth and board. Don't worry too much if the edges are slightly rough—the lip of the binding screw will cover these.

Japanese stab binding

A method commonly used in Japan and China, Japanese stab binding provides a simple sewn solution to binding single sheets of paper together. The visible, decorative sewing along the spine gives this binding its characteristic appearance.

This ancient binding method was used in China and Japan before the adoption of the codex. Rather than concealing the binding, the Japanese stab bind makes a feature of it. The simple, four-stitch pattern that grips the pages and covers together along the spine has become the central decorative element of the binding.

This binding can be achieved with very few tools and without the complex stitching required of multi-section folded bindings. It therefore offers an elegant solution to binding batches of single sheets, but has the flexibility to accommodate hard or soft covers and a vast range of materials. An established range of stitch patterns, from the traditional four-stitch pattern, through hemp leaf and tortoiseshell to the "noble" six-stitch pattern, extends the decorative choices available. Historically, if the book was of great importance, a larger number of stitch holes was used. In this project you will learn the basic principles of a four-stitch, soft-cover Japanese stab binding.

DEFINING CHARACTERISTICS

Single sheets of paper and cover material are bound together using a stitch pattern that holds the book block in a strong yet delicate bind. Little or no adhesive is required—it is the single length of thread that achieves rigidity in the spine.

Part of the margin is used to accommodate the stitch, so books made using this method will not lie flat when opened fully. To compensate for this lack of flexibility within the spine itself, it is advisable to use relatively lightweight paper, so that the paper offers as much flexibility as possible. Additionally, a soft, flexible cover is used, or, if a hard cover is required, a "hinge" can be built to allow it to open fully.

The binding's key feature is also one of its vulnerabilities: the stitch is on the outside and so is subject to wear and tear. For this reason a strong thread, traditionally silk, is always used and, in addition, can be threaded more than once through each anchor hole in the binding, if required.

Construction of a Japanese stab binding

A single piece of thread is sewn around the top, edges, and bottom of the book and tied off within the spine.

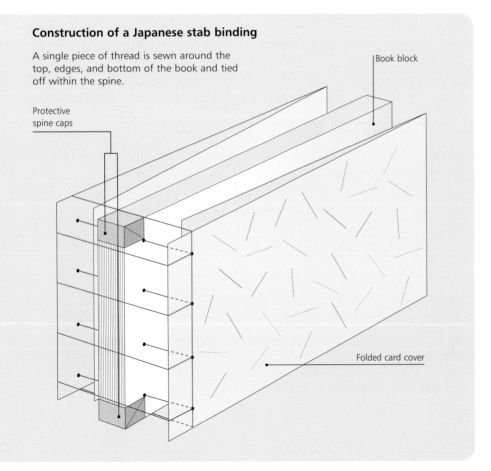

Protective spine caps

Book block

Folded card cover

Materials

- **Cover:** two sheets 110 lb (250 gsm) card, 8½ x 21 in. (21.5 x 53.3 cm), with grain parallel to the short edge
- **Book block:** 40 sheets 70 lb (100 gsm) paper, 8½ x 11 in. (21.5 x 28 cm)
- **Flyleaves:** two sheets 80 lb (130 gsm) paper, 8½ x 11 in. (21.5 x 28 cm)
- **Corner caps:** two sheets 80 lb (130 gsm) paper, 1 in. (2.5 cm) square
- PVA
- Strong upholstery thread or silk

Tools

- Pencil
- Ruler
- Bone folder
- Two bulldog clips
- Scrap wood or pieces of grayboard
- Awl
- Hammer
- Glue brush
- Scissors
- Needle

PREPARING THE BOOK BLOCK

Although there are many different variations of the Japanese stab-bound book, here you will learn one of the classic methods, using a four-hole traditional stitch, a doubled cover, and single sheets. If you are intending to use this book as a scrapbook, try using pages that are folded and therefore double, rather than single. This creates a little more bulk at the spine where the fold is, allowing you to glue items into your book later without causing too much bulking of the covers.

Step 1
On the reverse side of one of the cover sheets mark a fold point along the long edge at top and bottom at 11⅛ in. (28.2 cm). Score between these two points with a bone folder, then crease the card over. Repeat this for the second cover sheet.

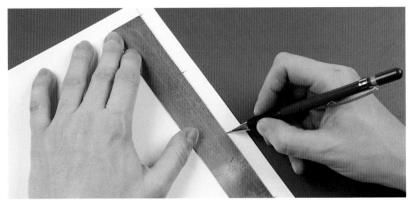

Step 2
The most accurate way to mark and punch the holes in your pages is to create a template for the punch marks. To do this, take one of your pages and mark a line ½ in. (12 mm) in from the spine edge, from top to bottom. Then, mark a point ½ in. (12 mm) from the top and bottom of the line—these will be your top and bottom stitch stations. Measure the distance between the top and bottom marks—your two final marks should divide this measurement into three.

> **NOTE:**
>
> You may need to divide the book block into two batches to ensure that the holes are punched accurately throughout.

Step 3
Take your pages, flyleaves, and cover sheets (with the non-folded, open edges at the spine) and tap the stack so that all pages are flush at the spine. Place the template so that the marked end of the sheet is flush with the spine and clamp bulldog clips around the book block. With a sheet of scrap wood (or pieces of grayboard) underneath the book to protect the work surface, use an awl and hammer to pierce each hole in turn, exactly where your markings are. Ensure that each and every hole is punched right through.

Step 4
Put the cover sheets to one side. Glue out one of the two small pieces of paper for the corner caps and, with your bulldog clips attached to the spine to keep it in place, attach the corner cap around the spine end, ½ in. (12 mm) down from the top of the spine and ½ in. (12 mm) along the top edge. Turn the "flaps" downward and glue them down so that they are flush with the spine—this requires two maneuvers, one to squash the protruding edges flat against the spine, the other to fold down the flaps—the last stage may require a dab of glue under the flaps. Clamp in place with bulldog clips and leave for five minutes. Repeat for the tail end of the spine.

Four-hole stitch order

When the stitch order is completed each stitch hole should have three entry/exit threads, except for the start/finish hole (marked), which will have four, including the first and last stitches.

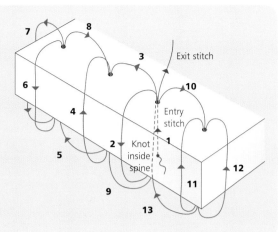

VARIATION

To create a tougher version of this book, try making a hinged, hard-bound top cover and a non-hinged back cover. Follow the principles used for the hard-bound cloth cover made when binding the hardback version of the post-bound book (see page 45), but use a hinge gap of ³⁄₁₆ in. (5 mm) rather than ³⁄₈ in. (1 cm).

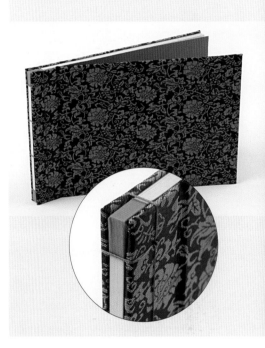

SEWING THE BOOK BLOCK

Step 1

Gather the pages and cover sheets and, ensuring that their spine edges are flush, reattach the bulldog clips at top and tail. Cut a length of strong thread about four times the length of your spine and thread it onto your needle. Push the needle through the second hole up from the back to the front of the book, leaving a tail of about 4 in. (10 cm).

Step 2

Separate the spine pages with your fingers and, using the awl, pull the tail end of your thread so that it hangs out of the middle of the spine stack. Take your thread end and tie a triple knot, then pull the other end of the thread through so that the knot is hidden in the spine. Trim any excess.

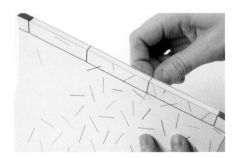

Step 3

Follow the thread order in the diagram (right) until you get to the final hole, keeping the thread taut at all times. Finish off by looping a knot in the thread by passing it under the first thread point and back down the final hole. This can then be trimmed off at the back.

Tying off

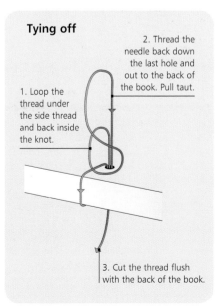

1. Loop the thread under the side thread and back inside the knot.

2. Thread the needle back down the last hole and out to the back of the book. Pull taut.

3. Cut the thread flush with the back of the book.

Dos-à-dos

The dos-à-dos, from the French for "back-to-back," binds two books within one cover or case. Although simple in structure, this binding allows the book to be divided into two distinct sections, offering the possibility of introducing contrasting or separate material within one book.

The methods by which two books are bound together can vary widely, but are often simple, depending on the materials being used and the strength of the binding required. At its simplest, the binding can be a pamphlet stitch or saddle stitch (staple), but more complex versions include spiral, wiro, stab, and perfect bindings. It is also possible to create a fully case-bound, multi-section version of the dos-à-dos.

The structure of this binding makes it ideal for making notebooks and journals, because the pages will lie flat when opened. The variety of methods that can be used to bind this type of book extends its versatility to make it one of the most interesting and yet accessible structures available to the bookmaker. Here, you will learn the fundamentals of a simple dos-à-dos notebook, and see how this can be extended to make a more complex case-bound version.

DEFINING CHARACTERISTICS

Strictly speaking, the dos-à-dos is a structure rather than a binding. It is possible to bind two books into one cover in a wide range of ways, but it is the back-to-back nature of the structure that makes it distinct and different from any other. The two book blocks share the same cover, but face in opposite directions, the fore-edge of one sitting next to the spine of the other. Depending on how you pick the book up, either of the two covers can be read as the front, so it is often necessary to make them different from each other so that they are immediately distinguishable.

The advantage of this structure is that it offers double the scope and double the number of pages of a normal structure, but this also makes the book slightly more difficult to handle than its more conventional relatives.

Construction of a dos-à-dos binding

Back-to-back construction

Pamphlet stitch binds the book block to the cover at the front and back

Z-shaped card acts as a cover for both books

See also

For an example of a notebook made using this technique, see *Bound to Argue* on page 106.

Materials

- **Cover:** one sheet 120 lb (270 gsm) card, 8 x 16 in. (20 x 40.6 cm), with grain parallel to the short edge
- **Book block:** 16 sheets 70 lb (100 gsm) paper, 8 x 10 in. (20 x 25.4 cm)
- **Endpapers:** two sheets 90 lb (180 gsm) paper, 8 x 10 in. (20 x 25.4 cm); choose different colors
- **Strong thread**

To make a case-bound version you will also need:
- **Mull:** two strips, 7½ in x 2 in. (19 x 5 cm)
- **Grayboard:** two sheets ⅛ in. (2 mm) thick, the same width as your book block and ⅜ in. (10 mm) taller; one sheet, ⅛ in. (3 mm) smaller than two sheets detailed above
- **Book cloth:** two pieces, width dependent on size of spine, 2 in. (5 cm) taller than the grayboard
- **Cover paper:** three sheets, the same width as your grayboard and 1 in. (2.5 cm) taller at the top and bottom
- **Scrap paper**
- **PVA/paste mix**

Tools

- Pencil
- Ruler
- Bone folder
- Awl
- Scissors
- Needle
- Scalpel, steel ruler, and cutting mat

To make a case-bound version you will also need:
- Glue brush
- Book weight or heavy, flat object

MAKING A DOS-A-DOS NOTEBOOK

Follow the steps below to make a pamphlet-stitched dos-à-dos notebook with two different-colored endpapers.

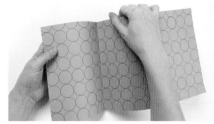

Step 1
Take the large cover sheet of card and mark where the folds will be, according to the diagram below.

Step 2
Accurately score the fold marks with a ruler and the tip of a bone folder, one on the back and one on the front. Crease the card so that the score marks lie inside the "V" of the fold.

Step 3
Fold the book block sheets and endpapers in half, parallel to the short edge, and gather them in two batches of eight sheets, stacking each one inside the next. Place an endpaper on the outside of each eight-sheet batch.

Step 4
Take one batch and position it inside one of the cover folds. Use a pencil to mark three stitch holes along the inside fold, starting at the center and equally dividing the spine along its length. Use an awl to pierce the holes through the paper and card, from the inside to the outside.

Step 5
Cut a length of strong thread about three times the length of your spine and thread it onto your needle. Starting on the outside, draw your thread through the center hole, leaving a tail of about 4 in. (10 cm) on the end of the thread, and sew a three-hole stitch (see page 22). Tie a reef knot (see page 23) and trim the thread to within 1 in. (2.5 cm) of the spine.

Step 6
Repeat Steps 4 and 5 to sew the second book block into the other cover. Use a scalpel and steel ruler to trim the excess card and paper so that the fore-edge of one book is flush with the spine of the other.

Marking and scoring the cover card

The excess card to the right and left of the cover sheet will be trimmed to size to complete the book.

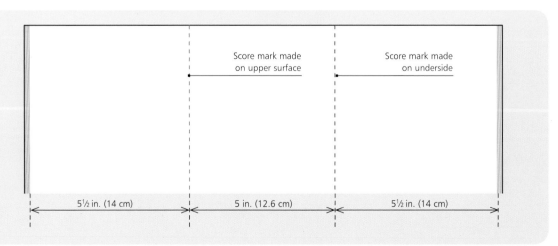

Score mark made on upper surface

Score mark made on underside

5½ in. (14 cm)   5 in. (12.6 cm)   5½ in. (14 cm)

MAKING A CASE-BOUND DOS-A-DOS BOOK

To make a hardback, case-bound version of the dos-à-dos it is necessary to construct the case using the quarter-bound method (see page 36) using both paper and cloth. It is not possible to use a full-cloth binding here because the two-way structure won't allow it.

Make your measurements according to the size of your book blocks. Your grayboard should be about $\frac{3}{16}$ in. (5 mm) larger at top and bottom than your book block, and the same width. However, the center piece of grayboard should be about $\frac{1}{8}$ in. (3 mm) smaller than the outer two to compensate for the two protruding spines.

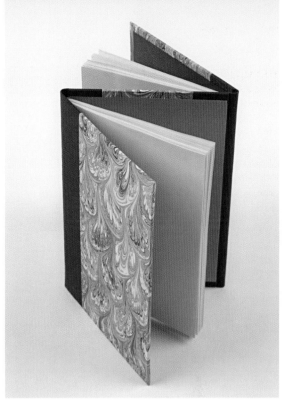

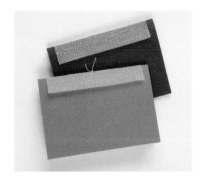

Step 1
Make your two book blocks according to the instructions for Preparing the book block of the single-section binding project (see page 26), not forgetting the addition of the mull to help attach the book block to the case.

Step 2
Make your case according to the structure shown in the diagram below. Keep to the principles of quarter-binding using both paper and cloth, where the cloth is laid down first, then the paper, which slightly overlaps the cloth.

Step 3
Case-in your book blocks in the usual way (see pages 27–28), the only difference being that you are casing-in two book blocks, one facing one way, the second facing in the opposite direction, within the "Z" structure of the case.

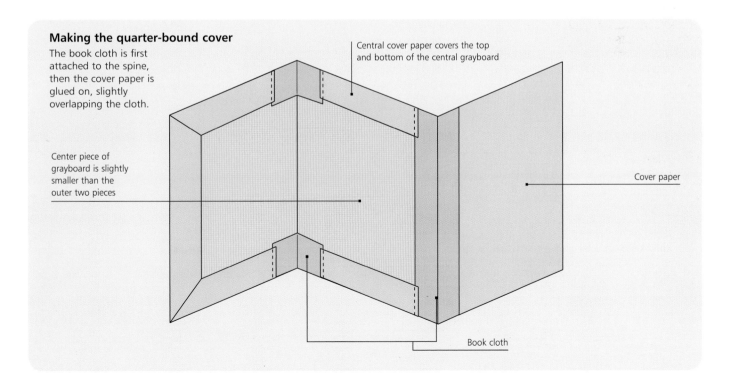

Making the quarter-bound cover
The book cloth is first attached to the spine, then the cover paper is glued on, slightly overlapping the cloth.

Central cover paper covers the top and bottom of the central grayboard

Center piece of grayboard is slightly smaller than the outer two pieces

Cover paper

Book cloth

Concertina binding

The concertina is a stitchless, folded binding that can be assembled with or without adhesive. It is easy to make and offers a versatility that can be creatively adapted to an enormous range of projects.

The concertina, or accordion binding, is an ancient binding method that sits somewhere between a modern sewn book and an ancient scroll. It was the first binding to take the book form—it can be read like a book, but its contents are displayed on one continuous folded sheet. Previously, concertinas would be limited to the size of a single sheet of paper, but contemporary versions are often made from a number of glued sections that overcome this limitation. This enables you not only to increase the size of your book, but also to change the

papers within the concertina at any point along its length. Here you will learn the principles of concertina binding, as well as one method of casing a concertina into a cover.

DEFINING CHARACTERISTICS
The concertina is made by the repeated, counter-folding of a sheet of paper—the flat surfaces between the folds constitute the pages. The folds allow the finished object to be held in the hand and read like a book, but when opened fully, the single sheet may be several feet long. By

its nature, the concertina book offers two distinct sides: the front, which is usually the side presented to the reader, and the back, which is often, although not always, left blank. The pages can be left unbound or can be cased either in a single board at front and back, or a case binding, similar to a sewn book.

See also
A Diction, on page 110, is a concertina book with an altered page shape.

Construction of a concertina binding

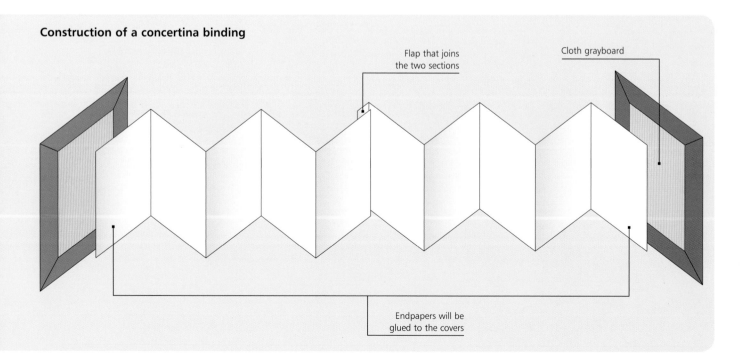

Flap that joins the two sections

Cloth grayboard

Endpapers will be glued to the covers

Materials

- **Book block:** one sheet 100 lb (220 gsm) paper, 3¾ x 18¾ in. (9.5 x 47.5 cm), with grain parallel to the short edge; one sheet 100 lb (220 gsm) paper, 3¾ x 19¼ in. (9.5 x 49 cm), with grain parallel to the short edge
- **PVA glue**
- **Book cloth:** two pieces, 6 x 6 in. (15 x 15 cm)
- **PVA/paste mix**
- **Grayboard:** two sheets ¹⁄₁₆ in. (2 mm) thick, 4 x 4 in. (10 x 10 cm)
- **Scrap paper**

Tools

- Pencil
- Ruler
- Bone folder
- Glue brush
- Scalpel, steel ruler, and cutting mat
- Book weight or heavy, flat object

MAKING THE CONCERTINA BOOK BLOCK

Follow the step-by-step instructions to create a concertina book block made from two strips of paper.

Marking the fold lines

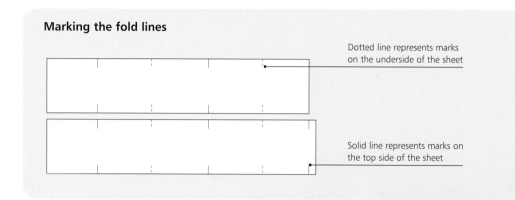

Dotted line represents marks on the underside of the sheet

Solid line represents marks on the top side of the sheet

NOTE:

If you are using thinner paper—for example, around 70–90 lb (100–180 gsm)—you can make all of your marks on the same side of the sheet, because it is less liable to crack along the score marks when folded the "wrong" way.

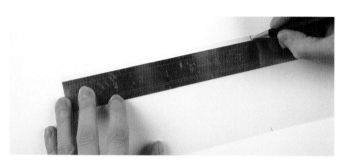

Step 1
Take the shorter sheet of paper and, with a pencil, mark the top and bottom edge of the sheet at 7½ in. (19 cm) intervals. Turn the sheet over and mark the back every 7½ in. (19 cm), but starting 3¾ in. (9.5 cm) in from the edge, so that the marks are positioned in between the marks on the other side. Repeat this on the second sheet of paper. You will be left with a ½ in. (12 mm) extra portion at the end of the second sheet, which will become the flap used to join the two sheets together.

Step 2
Use the end of a bone folder along a steel ruler to lightly score the paper between the points you have marked. This will ensure that your paper folds over easily and cleanly. Repeat on the second sheet.

Step 3
Start with the shorter strip and fold the first crease backward, the next crease forward, and carry on in this way until you have folded all the creases. Do the same with the second strip of paper. Your score marks should end up on the inside of the "V" of the fold—this will prevent the paper from cracking when folded.

Step 4
To join the two strips together to make a single sheet, lightly glue the inside of the short flap on your longer strip. Join the two parts together so that the short flap is behind the end of the shorter strip. Dry this joint under a flat, heavy weight for ten minutes. Use a scalpel and steel ruler to trim any paper protruding at the top or bottom of the join.

MAKING AND ATTACHING THE COVERS

Step 1

Glue out one of the book cloth pieces, starting from the center and working outward, then place a piece of grayboard at the center. Cut off the four corners of your glued book cloth to about ¼ in. (5 mm) from the corner point of the grayboard. With the aid of the steel ruler, fold the two opposite sides of the cloth onto the grayboard, and press firmly down.

Step 2

Tuck in the corners of the book cloth then fold over the remaining two sides. Again, press these firmly down. Repeat Steps 1 and 2 for the second cover board, and dry both covers under a flat weight for 20 minutes.

Step 3

With the concertina folded, place a sheet of scrap paper under the top sheet. Glue out this top sheet lightly but thoroughly.

Step 4

Pick up the glued end sheet of the concertina with both hands and lightly position it on the reverse of one of the cover boards. Once you are sure it is centrally placed on the cover, firmly press it in place. Repeat Steps 1 and 2 for the back cover.

VARIATION

It is also possible to bind your concertina into a single-piece, case-binding (see pages 28–29). Binding it in this way makes it easier to handle, but also allows you to obscure the reverse of the concertina and play with this concealment using cut-throughs or hidden text.

Flag book

The flag book is a simple but intriguing binding that lends itself to experimentation with image, shape, and color. Based on a concertina structure, this binding creatively utilizes the basic characteristics of the zigzag fold.

Invented by Hedi Kyle in the 1970s, this structure has been enthusiastically taken up by bookbinders and book artists alike. It utilizes the basic nature of the concertina fold—the fact that each consecutive face of the fold sits in the opposite direction from the next. When pages are added to each fold, half will face in one direction and half will face in the opposite direction. This is harnessed to great potential within this structure, creating a complex and dynamic visual experience. It is often used to create fragmented imagery, but just as easily lends itself to explorations with colors and form, allowing you to have fun with the nature of its visual display.

Here you will learn how to construct the basic flag book using colored papers, showing the effects when fully open and closed. You can then develop this experimentally using image and text.

DEFINING CHARACTERISTICS

Taking the concertina as its starting point, the flag book requires a much tighter, smaller fold—this fold acts as the extended spine of the book, onto which your pages, or "flags," are fixed in two different directions. When the concertina is extended fully, these added pages display themselves flat, creating a stepped or tiled panorama. When the concertina is closed, the pages stick out perpendicular to the spine, more resembling the traditional book. It is its dual nature that defines this binding and its potential for experimentation. The folding of the concertina needs to be extremely accurate, because any discrepancies will be magnified once the flags are added.

The flag book can be bound into hard or soft covers, but hard covers are more likely to protect the pages, which are vulnerable because they are cut into three or more parts.

Construction of a flag book
In this diagram a simplified, two-fold version of the flag book shows the basic structure of the flags attached to the concertina spine.

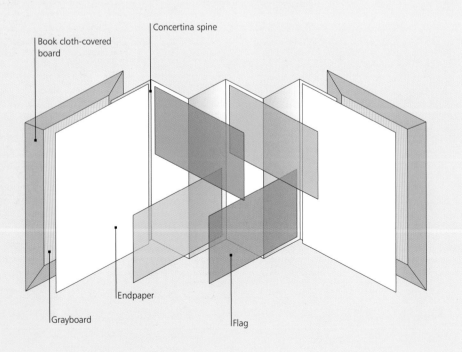

Book cloth-covered board

Concertina spine

Endpaper

Grayboard

Flag

See also
For more complex applications of this technique, see Karen Hanmer's flag book, *Destination Moon*, on page 117.

Materials

- **Spine:** one sheet 80–90 lb (140–180 gsm) paper, 6¼ x 16 in. (15.8 x 40.6 cm), with grain parallel to the short edge
- **Double-sided tape**
- **Flags:** 15 sheets 90–100 lb (180–220 gsm) paper, 2 x 5 in. (5 x 12.7 cm), three each of red, orange, yellow, green, and blue, with grain parallel to the long edge
- **Endpapers:** two sheets 80 lb (140 gsm) paper, 6¼ x 5 in. (16.5 x 12.7 cm)
- **Grayboard:** two sheets, ⅛ in. (2 mm) thick, 6¾ x 5½ in. (17.2 x 13.3 cm)
- **Book cloth:** two pieces, 1 in. (2.5 cm) larger than the grayboard on all sides
- **PVA/paste mix**
- **Scrap paper**

Tools

- Pencil
- Ruler
- Bone folder
- Glue brush
- Scalpel, steel ruler, and cutting mat
- Book weight or heavy, flat object

FOLDING THE NARROW CONCERTINA SPINE

Flag books using text or images need a good deal of planning and experimentation, but to illustrate the format's basic structure this project teaches the fundamentals of its construction and the effects of the page fragmentation using plain, colored pages.

Step 1

Take the spine sheet of paper and fold it in half parallel to the short edge. Then, fold each half in half again, lining up the edge of the paper with the center fold. Now fold the right edge across to the far left fold line, and crease it. Do the same on the opposite side. You should now have a sheet with four folds in the center half. Take the right edge and fold it to the nearest right-hand fold. Repeat on the other side of the sheet. You should now have a sheet divided into eight equal portions.

Step 2

To double the number of folds to sixteen, refer to the diagram, right as you fold. Fold the right-hand edge over to fold 1, and crease. Open up the sheet again and fold the right-hand edge over to fold 2. Then repeat the process for fold 3 and then fold 4. Flip the sheet around 180 degrees and follow the same fold pattern for folds 5, 6, 7, and 8. You should now have a sheet with 16 equal, folded portions. Finally, so that the folds are going the right way, refold the sheet along the fold lines so that the sheet forms an extended zigzag. As you will only need 12 of these 16 folded portions, trim off four of the portions on either the left or the right of the sheet.

Fold order, second stage

Fold the red edge over to folds 1, 2, 3, and 4 in turn, creasing as you go. Then, with the sheet turned 180 degrees, fold the blue edge over to folds 5, 6, 7, and 8. The dotted lines show the crease that each fold makes.

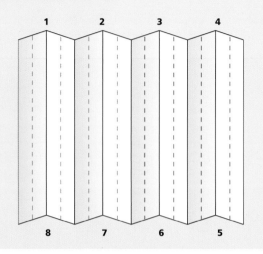

NOTE:

This half-fold method is the most accurate way of folding very narrow concertinas, rather than the marking, scoring, and folding method described on page 56. This method is suitable for folding a sheet in multiples of four folds.

INSERTING THE FLAGS

Step 1

Open out your folded sheet and make a faint pencil mark 2⅛ in. (5.4 cm) down the short edge at either end of the sheet. Then draw a very faint line between these marks, but only on folds 3, 5, 7, 9, and 11. These faint lines will act as your guides for the middle row of flags. Your top and bottom rows of flags will line up with the top and bottom of your sheet, respectively.

Step 2

Place a piece of double-sided tape at the end of each of your flags. Peel the release paper from the tape on the blue flag and position the flag in the second valley in from the right, ensuring it runs flush with the top edge of the concertina spine. The loose end of the flag should be to the right. Repeat this for each color in turn in each subsequent valley of your top row of flags.

Step 3
Peel the release papers from your second batch of colored flags and this time, starting from the left, position the red flag in the second valley, flush with the top of the pencil line. This time the loose end of the flag should be on the left. Repeat this for the other four flag stations on this row ensuring that all are exactly flush to the top edge of the pencil line, but that the line is not visible.

Step 4
Repeat the process for the bottom row of flags, mimicking the top row, but this time positioned flush to the bottom edge of the concertina spine. Once all are in place, open and shut the concertina a number of times to make sure that none of the flags catch on their neighbors and that the folds close and open properly.

Step 5
Attach a piece of double-sided tape to the length of the long edge of each endpaper, as close to the edge as possible. Peel the release papers and then attach the endpapers to each end fold of the concertina spine, on the inside. Press them firmly in place. Your flag book is now ready to case-in.

MAKING THE COVERS

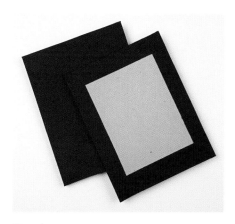

Step 1
Make your cover boards using grayboard and book cloth, as described on page 57.

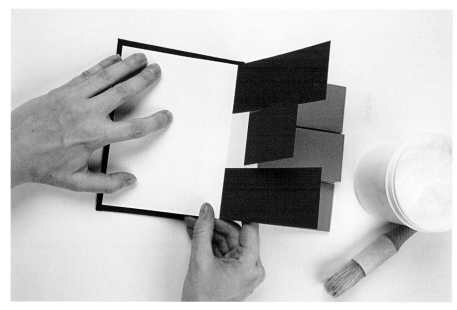

Step 2
Glue out the back of one of the endpapers, using scrap paper to prevent glue from getting on the rest of your book. Attach the endpaper centrally on the back of the prepared cover board, smoothing it down firmly once you are confident it is in the right position. Repeat for the back board.

NOTE:

Double-sided tape is less likely to buckle the paper than a liquid-based glue.

Tunnel book

A book format with a rich heritage, the tunnel book offers a three-dimensional space within the bounds of a simple, dual concertina structure.

During the Renaissance the fascination with perspective and optical experiments led to the exploration of perspective within boxes, where peepholes were used to view layered miniature scenes. By the sixteenth and seventeenth centuries, smaller and more portable versions emerged as peep shows, which were enthusiastically taken up by traveling entertainers at fairs and shows, where they would fascinate their audiences with depictions of historical, mythical, and biblical tales. It is likely that the collapsible, concertina sides of the tunnel book emerged as a way of making these books more portable, though this development did not come to light until the middle of the nineteenth century.

The modern tunnel book, therefore, has a rich and important history relating to both scientific understanding and creative storytelling. The structure can be adapted in a large variety of ways, although the basic construction always remains the same. In this project you will learn the principles of making a five-panel tunnel book with a case-bound cover.

DEFINING CHARACTERISTICS

The tunnel book is constructed using a series of upright, flat panels that are flanked and supported by a dual concertina. These panels attach to the folds of the concertina on each side, and can be cut in a variety of ways to create views and "scenes" right through to the solid back panel. The cut areas are usually larger on the front panel and decrease in area with each subsequent panel.

The concertinas allow the book to be closed flat, but also create the movable and three-dimensional space within which the scenes are set. The greater the size of the concertina folds, the greater the space between each panel, and with this comes a greater potential for both concealment and revelation.

Construction of a tunnel book

The back panel is attached to the inside of the back fold of each concertina, which is then attached to the inner face of the cover.

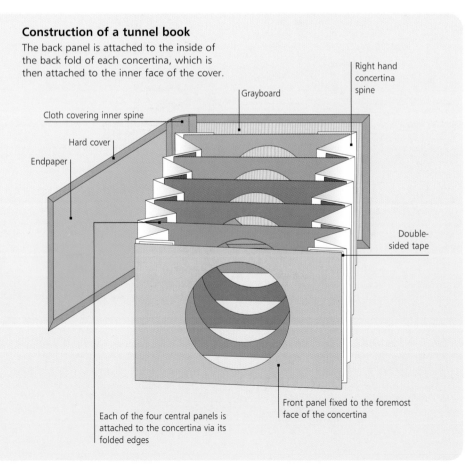

Cloth covering inner spine

Hard cover

Endpaper

Grayboard

Right hand concertina spine

Double-sided tape

Each of the four central panels is attached to the concertina via its folded edges

Front panel fixed to the foremost face of the concertina

See also

Another example of a tunnel book is Maria G. Pisano's *Tunnel Vision*, which can be found on page 118.

Materials

- **Central panels:** six sheets 90 lb (180 gsm) paper, 5½ x 7 in (14 x 18 cm), choose different colors
- **Concertina sides:** two sheets 80–90 lb (150–180 gsm) paper, 5½ x 16 in. (14 x 40.5 cm)
- **Double-sided tape**
- **Card strip for spine insert:** 120 lb (270 gsm) card, 5¾ x ½ in. (14.6 x 1.2 cm)
- **Book cloth:** enough for spine
- **PVA/paste mix**
- **Grayboard:** two sheets, 5¾ x 6¼ in. (14.6 x 15.7 cm)
- **Cover paper:** 8 x 16 in. (20 x 40.5 cm)
- **Scrap paper**
- **Endpaper:** one sheet 90 lb (180 gsm) paper, 5½ x 6 in (14 x 15 cm)

Tools

- Ruler
- Pair of compasses
- Scalpel, steel ruler, and cutting mat
- Bone folder
- Pair of compasses
- Glue brush
- Book weight or heavy, flat object

MAKING A FIVE-PANEL TUNNEL BOOK

The subject and nature of the cutout content for your panels is entirely a matter of choice, but here simple circles are used to show the basic effect of the three-dimensional space created within the tunnel.

Step 1
Fold the edges of your four central panels to provide a lip at each side to enable them to be glued to the concertina. Score a line ½ in. (1.2 cm) in from each short edge. Carefully crease each line using a ruler to help guide you. The front and back panels do not need a lip because they will be glued to the front and back fold of the concertina respectively, so simply trim ½ in. (1.2 cm) off the right and left edges of these.

Step 2
Using a pair of compasses, draw one circle onto each panel sheet except the back one, ensuring that they decrease in size, the largest being at the front. Use a scalpel to carefully cut them out. Make sure you do not cut within 1 in. (2.5 cm) of the edge or edge fold, otherwise the concertina will be visible when the panels are attached.

Step 3
Fold two concertinas following the instructions detailed on page 60. This will produce two concertinas, each with sixteen equal folds. For this project you only need twelve folds, so trim off the four unwanted folds on each concertina.

Step 4
To assemble your tunnel begin with the back, uncut panel. As with the flag book (see pages 58–61), the easiest way to attach your pages to the narrow concertinas is to use double-sided tape. Position tape on the inside of the back fold of your two concertinas, then peel off the release paper and carefully attach the back panel inside the last fold, pressing firmly to secure it in position.

Step 5
Tape the outside of the flaps of your four central panels, and attach these into the valley of the fold, with the panels' flaps facing backward. Make sure that you assemble them so that the cut circles get larger toward the front.

Step 6
Finally, apply tape to the very front fold of your two concertinas, then attach your front panel.

> **NOTE:**
> Before committing to a particular arrangement of cuts you can play about with their positioning by propping the series of panels up in line and viewing the results. Use jars or hardback books as your props.

GIVING THE TUNNEL BOOK A HARD COVER

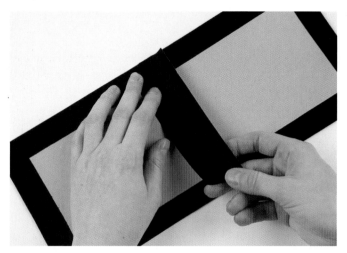

Step 1
Follow the instructions for making a case, as described in the section on multi-section case-binding (see pages 36–37). Start by finding the depth of the spine width by measuring how deep your tunnel book is when closed and flat—your spine insert should be slightly wider than this.

Step 2
The inside of the book will be visible, so cover the spine area with book cloth, making sure that you define the spine area with your bone folder. Dry this thoroughly under a flat weight before continuing.

Step 3
Add the endpaper to the front inside of your cover. The back will not need an endpaper because the back panel of your tunnel book will be attached to it.

Step 4
Using a glue brush, glue out the back of the back panel of your tunnel and attach it to the right-hand inside face of your case, pressing it firmly in position. Dry the book flat.

Carousel book

The carousel book is an elaborate variation on the concertina.
Although relatively simple to make, the carousel can be a very rich
and engaging format with great potential for visual storytelling.

The carousel book, also known as a star book, is made by joining three separate, differently sized concertinas together. When closed it sits flat like a normal book, but when opened fully it forms a visually intriguing shape that looks like a carousel from the side and a star when seen from above. The layers provided by the three concertinas are often richly exploited using cut-throughs from the outer layers to reveal three-dimensional, theater-like "scenes" that can be used to tell a visual story. As with the basic concertina, this format allows for the back surface of the folds to be further exploited to tell a text- or image-based story that links with the scenes, though more often this is left blank.

The format appeared in the 1950s, although it wasn't until the 1980s that the term "carousel" was coined. In this project you will be shown how to make a basic carousel book. Once these principles are understood, a great range of adaptations can be made to wonderful effect, involving extraordinarily elaborate cutout scenes and pop-ups.

DEFINING CHARACTERISTICS

The carousel usually contains between three and seven "scenes," the construction of which need to be well planned. A calculator, ruler, and protractor are essential for working out lengths and angles of the constituent parts. It is most often made using three differently sized concertina-folded sheets, each sheet having its own "face," or fold, size. These sheets are then joined together at the peak of their folds, which fixes their position in relation to each other. It is the different sizes of the faces of the folds that creates the three-dimensional space. The foreground and mid-ground are then cut into so that the layer behind is revealed—the foreground is usually cut to a greater extent than the mid-ground.

It is usual to use a lighter-colored paper for the outermost concertina and darker papers for the mid-ground and background layers, although this is not a fixed rule and there are many variations. The background layer is usually left uncut.

When the front and back covers of the joined concertinas are pulled backward and placed adjacent to each other, the structure transforms into a carousel, revealing the sequence of scenes. As there is a lot of energy in the folded sheets, it is necessary to tie the two covers together to prevent them from springing apart.

Construction of a carousel book
Three layers of concertina are sewn together and glued into two board covers.

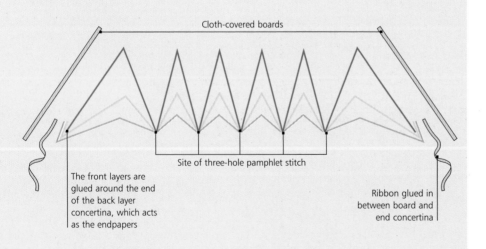

Cloth-covered boards

Site of three-hole pamphlet stitch

The front layers are glued around the end of the back layer concertina, which acts as the endpapers

Ribbon glued in between board and end concertina

See also
An intricate carousel book using detailed cutouts is featured on page 119.

Materials

- **Concertinas:** three sheets 80–90 lb (140–180 gsm) paper, in the following sizes:
  A: white, 4 x 17½ in. (10 x 44 cm)
  B: light green, 4 x 22 in. (10 x 56 cm)
  C: dark green, 4 x 31½ in. (10 x 80.4)
- **Strong thread**
- **Glue stick**
- **Grayboard:** ⅛ in. (2 mm) thick, 4⅛ x 2¾ in. (10.3 x 7 cm)
- **Scrap paper**
- **PVA/paste mix**
- **Book cloth:** 5½ x 4 in. (14 x 10 cm)
- **Ribbon:** ⅛ in. (3 mm) wide, two pieces, each 5 in. (13 cm) long

Tools

- **Pencil**
- **Bone folder**
- **Scalpel, steel ruler, and cutting mat**
- **Scissors**
- **Needle**
- **Two bulldog clips (optional)**
- **Glue brush**
- **Book weight or heavy, flat object**

PUTTING A CAROUSEL BOOK TOGETHER

Here you will learn how to make a six-scene carousel with a series of simple cutout scenes.

Step 1

To prepare the concertinas, first mark the fold lines at the top and bottom edges of the sheet. Sheets A and B will have extra fold flaps at each end that will attach to sheet C. Flip the paper over and start on the in-between folds, following the diagram, right.

Sheet A: fold marks to be at ½ in. (1 cm), then every 2¾ in. (7 cm) thereafter.

Sheet B: fold marks to be at ½ in. (1 cm), then every 3½ in. (9 cm) thereafter.

Sheet C: fold marks to be every 5¼ in. (13.4 cm).

Score these fold marks with the point of a bone folder, then crease each one so the point of the fold is away from you. You now have half your folds in place. Then you need to fold the in-between folds, see diagram, right.

Folding the in-between folds

Fold crease A over to points 1, 2, and 3, creasing at each point. The red dotted lines show the folds that will be created. Turn the sheet 180 degrees and repeat for crease B, folding it over to points 4, 5, and 6 and creasing at each stage. The blue dotted lines show the folds that will be created. Remember to ignore the edge lip folds (marked in green; these will be on sheets A and B but not C)—you are not folding the edge of the paper.

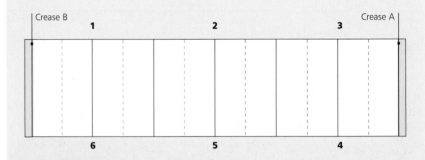

Step 2

Make templates to help you make simple cuts in your foreground and mid-ground sheets. For each template, cut out sheets of card equal in size to two folds of your concertina. Decide on the shape you would like to use—here, a star is used, but the shape could be anything you choose. With more elaborate carousels, each scene can be different. For the foreground template, draw or measure your shape onto the piece of card, then cut the shape out with a scalpel. Repeat this for your mid-ground shape, making it smaller than the foreground one. If you are using the same basic shape, use your larger template as a guide to judge the outline of the smaller template.

Step 3

Take your smallest (foreground) concertina and place your largest template over the first double fold, then draw around it. Repeat this for each double fold in turn, and then carefully cut out the shape you have drawn, ensuring that you cut on the outside of the pencil line, otherwise this will be visible when the carousel is finished. Then take your mid-ground concertina and draw and cut out your shapes in the same way, using the smaller template. The background concertina needs no cutting.

Step 4

Assemble the three concertinas so that each consecutive fold of one sits in each fold of the next, as shown in the diagram on page 66. To fix the three concertinas together, mark out a three-hole pamphlet stitch on the back of the first set of folds, following the instructions on page 22. Starting from the inside of the fold, complete the three-hole stitch as detailed on page 22—do not start on the outside. Tie off with a reef knot and trim the thread ends to 1 in. (2.5 cm).

Repeat this step for each of the five joints, so that you end up with the three concertinas attached at the five points throughout their length.

Step 5

To complete this part of the carousel you need to glue the end flaps of the fore- and mid-ground sheets onto the background sheet, at both ends. The cloth-bound covers will be attached to these.

Apply glue from a glue stick to the back of the mid-ground end flap and attach it to the outside of the end of the background sheet, pressing firmly and accurately in place. Repeat this for the foreground flap and glue this over the mid-ground flap you have just glued. If necessary, hold these joints in place with bulldog clips.

MAKING AND ATTACHING THE COVERS

Step 1

Make your cover boards using grayboard and book cloth, as described on page 57.

Step 2

To make ties for the covers, apply PVA to the end 1 in. (2.5 cm) of each piece of ribbon and place each glued end at the center of the fore-edge of the board. Press these down firmly and allow to dry for five minutes.

Step 3

Holding the carousel inside the end fold, carefully glue the endpaper, using scrap paper to protect other surfaces, and attach the carousel to one of your covers, making sure that the ribbon sits adjacent to the white, foreground sheet. Repeat for the other end of the carousel. Press the covers in place firmly and dry them with the book closed and flat under a weight.

Flip book

A flip book contains a sequence of related images that, when flipped by the reader's thumb, creates a miniature moving picture. All books rely on interactivity, but with the flip book this interactivity is absolutely essential to bring the book's contents to life.

Patented in the 1880s, the flip book owes its magic to a physiological phenomenon called "persistence of vision." The eye retains an image on the retina for about one-twelfth of a second. When the eye is exposed to a sequence of images at a rate faster than twelve per second it can't keep up with such a rapid change and will automatically join these images together, as each subsequent image will be superimposed over the previous one left on the retina. If, between each image, there is only a slight sequential change,

then the optical effect is one of smooth, constant motion. Persistence of vision is used to great effect in the creation of animation, movies, and, of course, the flip book. In fact, the flip book has historically been used by animators for testing short sequences.

Content for a flip book can be drawn, photographed, or extracted from video footage. Flip books are not difficult to make, but require good planning, an eye for detail, and plenty of trial and error. Here you will be guided through

the basic principles of creating your own flip book animation based on creating the illusion of a bouncing ball.

DEFINING CHARACTERISTICS

Flip books need to be easy to hold in two hands and small enough to flip through with the thumb. You need to plan for a minimum of twelve pages per second—a book with a two-second duration will give a strong sense of motion, although it is possible to create longer books. You need to achieve a balance between getting enough visual change between each image, but not so much that the motion appears jumpy. Bearing in mind a constant flip speed, the general principle is that fast motion requires fewer drawings and that slow motion requires a greater number of drawings.

It is important to keep content to the right-hand side of each page, because this is the most visible to the eye when the book is flipped. The paper that is used is also important, and needs to have enough bounce so that when flipped, the pages instantly move out of the way of the next image. The optimum paper is between 75 and 85 lb (120 and 160 gsm), with a relatively smooth finish and the grain parallel to the long edge.

The collection of single pages that constitute the flip book can be bound in a number of ways. This can be achieved very simply with a stapler, or in a more sophisticated way using perfect binding (see pages 38–41) with the addition of screw posts or tape.

Construction of a flip book

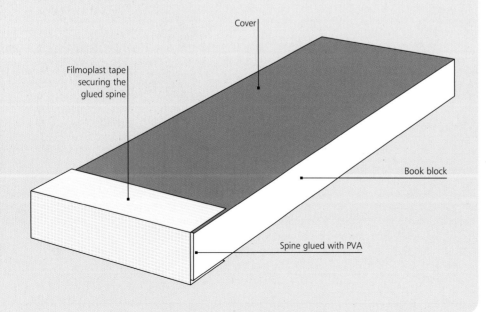

Cover

Filmoplast tape securing the glued spine

Book block

Spine glued with PVA

Materials

- **Planning paper:** several sheets of plain, 60 lb (70 gsm) paper, cut into 24 pages measuring 2 x 3½ in. (5 x 9 cm)
- **Book block:** several sheets of 80 lb (140 gsm) paper, white or colored, with grain parallel to the long edge
- **Glue stick**
- **Cover:** two sheets 90 lb (180 gsm) paper, 2 x 3½ in. (5 x 9 cm)
- **PVA glue**
- **Adhesive Filmoplast cloth:** 2 x 1 in. (5 x 2.5 cm), any color

Tools

- Pencil
- Bulldog clip
- Fine black pen
- Colored pencils
- Access to a photocopier
- Scalpel, steel ruler, and cutting mat
- Guillotine
- Two pressing boards
- Vise or two G-clamps
- Glue brush

MAKING A FLIP BOOK

This small flip book will be 24 pages in length and will animate a ball bouncing toward the reader. Although there are many different ways to create a flip book, here are some fundamental tips and techniques for developing smooth animation.

Step 1

On plain paper, plan the sequence of your animation so that you know the scope of the movement you are trying to create and what changes will occur to the objects from start to finish. It is worth spending some time studying how a ball does actually bounce, so that the process of translating this to a line drawing is a little easier. Plan this aspect of your animation in the form of a storyboard. You can either do this in full—24 frames—or abbreviate the storyboarding to map just the stages of change within the animation.

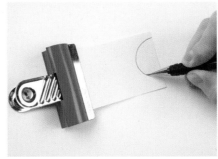

Step 2

Once you are confident of the journey your object will take from the beginning to the end of the animation, you can begin drawing onto your 60 lb (70 gsm) paper. Draw with a fine pen that creates a clean black line, making sure that the main focus of the drawing is on the right-hand side of the page. Draw the last page of your sequence first and work toward the beginning. You will find that the thin paper allows you to see the exact position of the animation on the next page, and with this in mind you may even prefer to use tracing paper.

> **NOTE:**
> As you begin each new page, insert it into a bulldog clip with the other drawn pages behind it, ensuring that they are exactly lined up with one another. This gives you the opportunity to flip through the pages at each and every stage to test that your animation is working, but also ensures that each page is perfectly registered—lined up—with the next.

Step 3

Continue working to the front of the book, page by page, checking all the time that your page progression matches the sequence in your storyboard. This will take practice, so don't be afraid to draw and redraw a number of times before you are happy with the result. Once you have all your pages drawn, you may wish to color them to bring them to life a little.

Step 4

To transfer the images to a heavier paper stock that will be more suitable for flipping, first take some spare paper and mark out a grid of boxes that are slightly larger than your book's pages—in this case, boxes of 2⅛ x 3⅝ in. (5.3 x 9.3 cm). Use a glue stick to stick each of your drawn pages close to the top right-hand corner of each box, numbering the sequence at the far left-hand side. Ensure that each page is glued in exactly the same position in relation to its box and is straight. This will help you register them accurately after photocopying so that the alignment of the drawing is not lost.

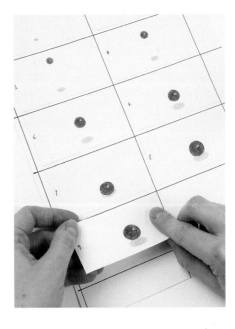

NOTE:

Photocopying your pages allows you to make several copies of your book and also translates the pen or pencil lines into lines that better resemble print.

Step 5

Photocopy the sheets onto the heavier paper then trim each page along the grid lines to create a page that can be trimmed down to the final size later. Ensure that you do this as accurately as possible.

Step 6

Reassemble all the pages in order and attach a bulldog clip to the fore-edge. Trim the spine edge with a scalpel.

NOTE:

Any method that is suitable for binding single sheets can be used to bind the flip book. These can include: a simple staple, a Japanese stab binding, or a post binding, all of which are described in this book.

Step 7

Bind the pages using the perfect binding method, adding covers at front and back (see pages 38–41). Once perfect-bound, trim the head, tail, and fore-edge so that all grid lines are trimmed off and ensure that, most importantly, the fore-edge is perfectly flush—crucial for smooth flipping. Try to use a heavy-duty guillotine for this final fore-edge trim, it is the easiest method and produces the best results.

Portfolio binding

The portfolio is a strong but flexible storage binding that can accommodate a wide variety of materials in a range of sizes. Although there are many versions of portfolio design, they are all built for a similar purpose—to store and carry loose, flat material, such as drawings, prints, and paintings.

Portfolios are easy to make and can be adapted to any size—the only change needed being the relative strength of the constituent materials. Their capacity, or depth, can also be adapted but needs to be relatively strong, because the weight of the portfolio's contents will sit on the main spine.

Begin by deciding on the size of your contents and design the elements of your portfolio with this in mind, allowing enough capacity so that they are not too tightly contained. If you have a variety of contents, simply design to their biggest dimensions.

DEFINING CHARACTERISTICS

Portfolios are constructed in a similar way to a hardback book cover. They are often made using grayboard and a combination of book cloth and cover paper, where the book cloth is used in the hinge area for strength and flexibility. Inner flaps are added to stop the contents from spilling out of the sides of the portfolio, and can either be integral, within an all-in-one construction, or made separately and fixed into the case. Ribbons are added to tie the back and front of the portfolio together, to help contain the contents snugly. Ribbons that have a large linen or cotton content are most suitable, because they provide adequate grip when tied—silky or nylon ribbons are liable to slip.

The portfolio design can be scaled up and down as necessary, but materials should be adapted accordingly.

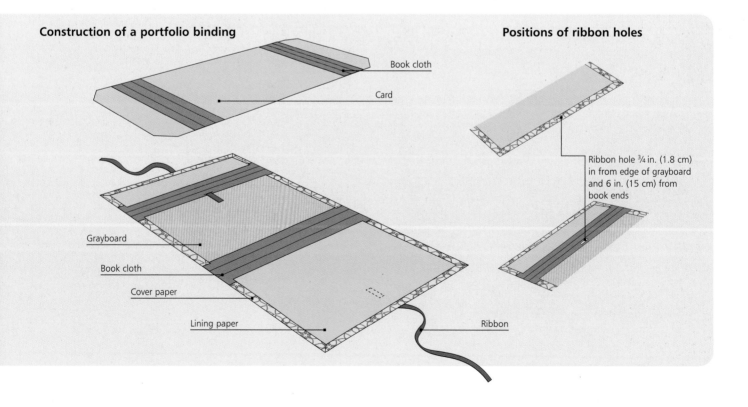

Construction of a portfolio binding

Book cloth

Card

Grayboard

Book cloth

Cover paper

Lining paper

Ribbon

Positions of ribbon holes

Ribbon hole ¾ in. (1.8 cm) in from edge of grayboard and 6 in. (15 cm) from book ends

Materials

See Component parts diagram (page 76)

- **Card:** 120 lb (270 gsm),
  A & C = 4 x 9in.
  (10 x 23 cm)
  B = 9 x 12 in.
  (23 x 30.5 cm)
- **Book cloth:**
  1 & 2 = 4 x 11 in.
  (10 x 28 cm)
  3 & 4 = 4 x 8¾ in.
  (10 x 22.2 cm)
  5 & 6 = 4 x 14½ in.
  (10 x 37 cm)
  7 & 8 = 4 x 12½ in.
  (10 x 32 cm)
- **Grayboard:** ⅛ in.
  (2 mm) thick,
  Y & Z = 9¼ x 12½ in.
  (23.5 x 32 cm)
  X = 4 x 12½ in.
  (10 x 32 cm)
- **Cover paper:**
  D = 14½ x 4 in.
  (37 x 10 cm)
  E = 14½ x 7¼ in.
  (37 x 18.5 cm)
  F = 14½ x 12½ in.
  (37 x 32 cm)
- **Cotton or linen ribbon:**
  9 & 10 = 12 in.
  (30 cm) lengths of ½ in.
  (10 or 12 mm)
  wide ribbon
- **Lining paper:** 80 lb
  (140–150 gsm), the
  same color as your
  inner card,
  G = 12¼ x 9 in.
  (31 x 23 cm)
  H = 12¼ x 3¾ in.
  (31 x 9.5 cm)
- **PVA/paste mix**
- **Scrap paper**
- **PVA glue**

Tools

- Pencil
- Steel ruler
- Glue brush
- Bone folder
- Book weights
  or heavy, flat objects
- Scalpel and
  cutting mat
- Chisel with ½ in.
  (1.2 cm) blade and
  hammer (optional)

MAKING THE INNER SECTION

For this project the portfolio's inner flap section and outer case are made separately and brought together at the end.

Component parts

For details of measurements for the component parts, see Materials on page 75.

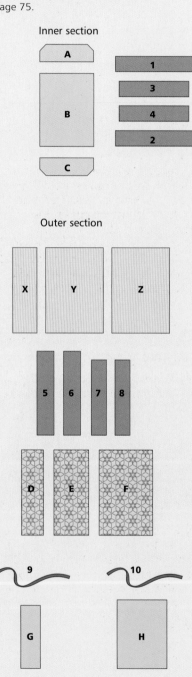

Inner section

A

1

3

B

4

2

C

Outer section

X

Y

Z

5 6 7 8

D E F

9   10

G

H

Step 1

Assemble the materials for the inner section (see left). These will be referred to by their letter or number. Take strips 1 and 2 of the book cloth and mark the lines where the sheets of card will sit when glued. Mark one line 1½ in. (3.8 cm) in from one long edge and another 1½ in. (3.8 cm) in from the other long edge.

Step 2

Glue out the back of strip 1 then position card B on the glued book cloth, abutting one of the marked lines. Take sheet A and position it along the other line, ensuring that the book cloth protrudes by equal amounts at both ends. Turn down the protruding book cloth and smooth it firmly front and back. Repeat for sheet C and strip 2.

Step 3

Glue the back of strip 3 and position the cloth on the reverse side of the inner section, so that it covers the gap, lining it up carefully with the end of the first piece of book cloth, and sitting just short of the edge of the card. Repeat this for strip 4 at the other end of the card, and smooth down.

MAKING THE OUTER SECTION

Step 1

Take strip 5 of book cloth and mark in pencil where the boards will sit once glued. This is not exactly the same as the capacity, because it needs to be slightly bigger to accommodate the inner section. So, mark a line just less than 1½ in. (3.8 cm) in from one long edge and a line the same distance from the other long edge, so that the inner gap is about 1⅛ in. (2.8 cm)—this will also accommodate the thickness of the grayboard.

Step 2

Glue out the reverse of one of the book-cloth strips and position sheet Y of grayboard against the line, ensuring that there are equal amounts of book cloth protruding at each end. Turn over the protruding book cloth and firm it in place. Position the smaller sheet X of grayboard against the second line. This is the top fore-edge flap of your portfolio and will be uppermost when it is carried or stored.

BRINGING THE INNER AND OUTER SECTIONS TOGETHER

Step 3

Mark up strip 6 of book cloth, but this time with a slightly larger gap than before, because this will have to accommodate not only the inner section but also the fore-edge flap. Mark at 1⅜ in. (3.5 cm) in from both long edges, so that the gap is 1¼ in. (3.1 cm). Glue out the back of the cloth and position the long end of grayboard sheet Y abutting the first line, again ensuring that there are equal amounts of book cloth protruding at both ends. Position board Z abutting the second line. Glue out the remaining book-cloth strips 7 and 8, and position them carefully in line with the existing book cloth so that they cover the two joints, as shown.

Step 4

Each section of grayboard now needs to be covered with paper. Take sheets D and F and glue out their backs. In turn, position each in place with ⅛ in. (3 mm) overlapping the book cloth at one edge, with the other edge protruding from the three other edges of the grayboard. With each, diagonally cut the two corners of paper. As you have done before in making the quarter-bound case for the multi-section binding (see pages 36–37), turn over the long edge of paper first and then nip in the corners, allowing you to then turn down the two remaining edges of paper. Glue out the remaining sheet of cover paper, E, and position it over the central grayboard area, overlapping each book-cloth edge by about ⅛ in. (3 mm). Turn down the two edge flaps of paper and smooth in place.

Step 1

You will now line the two outer sections of grayboard—the central section will not need lining because it will be covered. The lining will not only cover the grayboard, but will also obscure the ends of the ribbon. Glue out the back of sheets G and H and position them carefully over the grayboard so that they are about ⅛ in. (3 mm) from the edges. Smooth them down firmly, ensuring that the area around the ribbon is as flat as possible. Dry the folder open with flat weights and scrap paper.

Step 5

Mark holes for the ribbons at the positions indicated on the diagram (see page 74). Working from the outside of your portfolio, cut neat slits right through the grayboard and cover paper, using either a scalpel or a chisel and hammer, depending on the thickness of the grayboard. The width of your slits should be equal to the width of your ribbon. From the outside, insert a piece of ribbon in each slit so that about 1 in. (2.5 cm) is inside the portfolio. Glue down the ribbon end with PVA, pressing it so that it is as flat as possible. Repeat for the other ribbon position.

Step 2

Finally, the two elements of the portfolio can now be fixed together. Take your inner section and glue out the back of the central area, up to the first hinge gap on each side. Then, position the glued section on top of the central area of your outer section on the inside.

This chapter looks at different ways of treating the pages and covers of books. These elements provide the blank slate onto which you can stamp your personal style. They can be altered in a vast range of ways, and illustrated here are some basic techniques for achieving a small but fundamental range of effects. Basic principles and processes are outlined, and, once mastered, can be built on and adapted to your own projects.

CHAPTER TWO: page and cover

Cutting and layering paper

Cutting and layering the page can be a very effective decorative technique that makes the most of the multi-layered, sequential nature of the book.

Originating in China before the sixth century, paper cutting—cutting flat sheets of paper, sometimes several at once, with either scissors or an extremely sharp knife—has had a long and rich history. The Chinese created extraordinarily intricate paper cuts for both decorative and religious purposes. The Japanese developed origami into kirigami, where cuts are used in addition to folds. The popularity of paper cutting spread over the subsequent centuries and by the eighth century had reached western Asia. It was not seen in Europe until the sixteenth century, but has thrived in a number of forms since then. Before the widespread use of cameras, one very popular application was the silhouette, a small, simple framed portrait cut from black paper to the likeness of the sitter.

Paper cuts can now be found across the globe, with particularly strong traditions in Germany, Mexico, Poland, Japan, and the US, and are still generally used for creative and decorative purposes. Developments in technology, such as die and laser cutting, have opened up the possibility of cutting in large quantities

and with extreme intricacy, without the need for time-consuming work by hand, although both techniques have their limits too.

The application of paper cutting within the book form is a more limited but growing area, and here you will learn techniques and tips for creating books where page cutting is a central feature.

DEFINING CHARACTERISTICS

Although most paper cutting has been conceived, until recently, in flat sheet form, it is not difficult to imagine the potential of this art form if applied to the multiple, sequential pages of a book, where layers of cut paper can be built to create complex scenes. Page cutting can be applied to any book form to create decorative or narrative content without the need for print or image, but is particularly suited to the concertina form and single-section and single-leaf bindings, as well as more complex structures such as carousel and tunnel books. Scalpels and similar ultra-sharp knives are best for accuracy and intricacy, but blades need to be replaced regularly

so that you are always cutting with a fresh, sharp point. Most cutting is done freehand, but where there are straight lines it is advisable to use a steel ruler as a guide.

Although techniques for paper cuts within the book form are broad and wide-ranging, always consider the following points when planning a cut series of pages: plan your content thoroughly with the use of templates, drawn guides, and mock-ups; always use a cutting mat under your cut surface; always use a sharp blade to avoid tearing the page or making ragged cuts; always cut in good light; consider using layering as a by-product of making cuts—cuts will always reveal what is below or behind them, so think how this can be used to best effect; consider varying the color of your paper to create foreground and background effects; and consider safety at all times.

Materials

- Five sheets 90 lb (175 gsm) paper, 8 x 5½ in. (20 x 14 cm)
- One sheet 90 lb (175 gsm) paper, 8 x 27½ in. (20 x 70 cm)

Tools

- Cutting mat
- Scalpel and spare blades
- Eraser
- Sharp, light pencil

CREATING A CUT-PAGE BOOK

This cut concertina book is made from one sheet folded into five equal panels. First of all
you need to plan how your panels will be cut and how each will relate to the next.

Step 1

Initially, plan your five panels on five separate sheets, each the size of a
single panel. This allows you to adjust the cut design on each with much
more flexibility than if you were to plan it on the concertina. Consider the
elements that will be in the foreground and the background of this five-panel
scene. Cut the front panel, then draw your design onto the second panel,
then cut this. Cut then draw in turn until you get to the back panel.

Step 2

On your large sheet, place a mark every 5½ in. (14 cm) at top and bottom
along the long edge. These are your fold points. Score between these points
with the end of a bone folder, then crease each fold so that the front fold is
on the right and the back fold on the left, as shown.

Step 3

With a very light pencil line, transfer
each cut design onto your concertina,
page by page, using each as a
template to draw around.

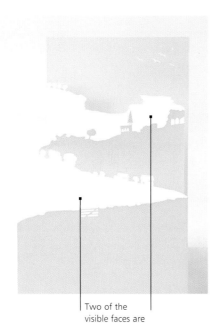

Two of the visible faces are on the reverse of the sheet.

NOTE:

- Remember, because of the nature of the concertina, it is the back of the second and fourth panels that will be on show once complete, so either draw around your template on the reverse of your concertina on these two panels, or flip the second and fourth templates around horizontally, and draw the mirror image on the front of the concertina.

- When designing your cut area, remember that one part of the cut image always needs to be attached to the rest of the page.

- Move the page around so that it is always positioned at the best angle for cutting.

- Cut on the "good" side of the line—the part that will be kept—so that there are fewer pencil lines to erase once completed.

- When cutting corner areas, cut away from the corner rather than toward it. This will create a clean, sharp corner cut.

VARIATION

In this alternative, cut sheets have been arranged within a single-section pamphlet-stitched book. Dark and light pages have been alternated to provide maximum contrast between the cut page and the background.

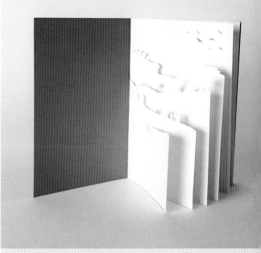

Step 4

Carefully cut each panel in turn, including cutting the birds into the fifth panel. Finally, with an eraser, gently rub away any remaining pencil marks from the edge of the cut lines.

Surface sculpting

Surface sculpting offers a way of creating a raised or sunken impression on the surface of a book's cover without the need for any expensive or specialist tooling.

This technique can be used to title or decorate the covers of your books. It involves either raising or sinking the surface of the cover using cut card between the board and cover material. The edges of the cut areas are then carefully defined using a pointed bone folder.

To create the appearance of a raised surface, the text or pattern is cut from card and added to the surface, creating a "positive" image. To create the appearance of a sunken surface, a full sheet of card is added to the cover, with the text or pattern cut away, creating a "negative" image.

DEFINING CHARACTERISTICS

The technique can be used on any book cover that uses a cover material over grayboard or millboard. It requires a relatively sturdy, flat base onto which the additional card is glued. Using "positive" and "negative" techniques together, it is possible to have areas that are both raised and sunken on the same cover. You can adjust the amount of relief—the depth of the raised or sunken area—by altering the thickness of card that you use, including having areas of different levels of relief. However, the amount of relief is limited by the elasticity or flexibility of your cover material, which gets stretched over or into the added or subtracted card.

This technique is most suited to relatively bold areas of text or pattern. It is possible to sculpt more detailed relief but it is more difficult to achieve good results with just a normal bone folder. Patterns and text can be created either by freehand drawing or using computer text and layout software.

Surface sculpting
For sunken areas, the added card acts as the finished surface into which you cut your text or pattern.

Cut card

Card letters

Grayboard

Cut letters are simply glued to the surface of the grayboard

Grayboard

Materials

- Card: one sheet 120 lb (270 gsm), 5¼ x 5¾ in. (13.5 x 15 cm)
  one sheet 95 lb (200 gsm), 5¼ x 5¾ in. (13.5 x 15 cm)
- Grayboard: two sheets, 5¼ x 5¾ in. (13.5 x 15 cm)
- PVA glue
- Silicone release paper
- Book cloth: one piece, 7 x 15 in. (18 x 37 cm)
- Paste/PVA mix

Tools

- Computer and printer, or pen
- Scalpel and cutting mat
- Scissors
- Glue brush
- Steel ruler
- Pressing board
- Book weight or heavy, flat object
- Pointed bone folder

CREATING A SCULPTED CASE-BOUND COVER

Here you will be shown how to create both raised and sunken areas on a case-bound cover, suitable for casing-in a single- or multi-section notebook.

Step 1

First, you need to create the artwork for your card cutouts. For this project there will be a raised area of text on the front cover and a sunken area of pattern on the back cover. You can either lay out your text or pattern in a computer program and print it directly onto the card, or hand draw it directly onto the card. For the front cover print or draw the text directly onto the 120 lb (270 gsm) card. Draw or print the pattern for the back cover on the sheet of lighter card.

Step 2

Carefully cut out the letters for the front cover using a scalpel on a cutting mat. Ensure you cut as accurately along the lines as possible. Keep the cutouts and discard the background, or save it to create a sunken area of text in another project. Now cut out the pattern for your back cover, this time keeping in mind that it is the background you need to keep.

NOTE:

When tackling intricate areas of text that need very precise positioning, print out your text onto a piece of light card the same size as your cover and glue this in place on the grayboard. This then acts as a guide for positioning each cutout letter.

Step 3

Apply a thin layer of PVA glue to the back of each letter for the front cover, ensuring that you glue right to the edges. Position each letter on one grayboard sheet, then cover the sheet and card with silicone release paper, a pressing board, and a weight to keep the cover flat while the glue dries, and ensure that the letters are firmly fixed in place.

Step 4

Because the pattern on the back cover is formed from what remains after cutting out the card, there is a far larger area of card to glue. For this reason it is usually easier to put a thin layer of glue over the whole of the grayboard sheet, then place the cut card in position over this. The layer of glue must be even and fine, because any lumps will show through once it is covered with book cloth.

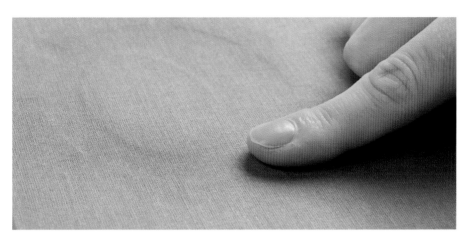

In this example a combination of raised and sunken sculpting has been used on the same cover.

Step 5

You are now ready to cover your grayboard with book cloth. Glue out your book cloth (see Step 1, page 27) using a PVA/paste mix. Place the two covers onto the glued book cloth, with the cut card facing down, the front cover to the left, and the back cover to the right. Ensure that your covers are orientated the right way, making sure you leave a spine gap to allow room for the book block (see Measuring the spine gap, page 27). Cut the corners of the cloth and turn in the sides with the assistance of a steel ruler (see Step 2, page 27). Turn the cover over so that the outside is now facing you, and carefully smooth down the book cloth with a flat palm to iron out any pockets of air. Define the areas of text and pattern with the soft tip of your finger—this should just help you locate exactly where the cut areas are below the cloth.

Step 6

Before the glue dries, use the point of a bone folder to define every edge of cut card that is under the book cloth. To do this, angle the point of the bone folder at about 45 degrees to the cut edge and work carefully along the ridge or valley. For the text on the front the ridge will be raised, and for the pattern on the back, sunken. This should be a slow, careful process, and you may need to go over the edges more than once. It will also be helpful to refer to a copy of your original artwork to check exactly where the edges of the card are. A prepared book block can now be cased into the sculpted cover.

Debossing

Debossing is a process by which a metal block or die is pressure-stamped into the surface of your work, leaving a permanent sunken impression of the design.

Often reserved for the professional bookmaker and leather worker, debossing (sometimes confusingly called embossing) is a simple yet versatile way of creating a shallow, sunken impression in the surface of a soft material such as paper, card, or leather. Debossing creates a finish that is similar to, but far more precise, than surface sculpting (see page 84). To impart the impression a metal die is pressed flat into the surface under the pressure of a G-clamp or specialist press.

Debossing is ideal for titling work or creating small areas of pattern or text on a cover or page. The impression created is "blind," with no print or ink, it's simply a sunken area matching your artwork. It is possible to create sunken areas that are printed, but this requires you to print first, then deboss precisely over the printed area, which is often very difficult to do without specialist equipment.

It is also possible to deboss without the use of a metal die, although objects used in place of it need to be chosen carefully, and the end result will be far less precise. Here you will learn how to create and commission a metal die for debossing a small blind impression into the cover of a notebook.

DEFINING CHARACTERISTICS

A debossed impression creates a shallow, clean-lined imprint in your chosen surface. There is a limit to the amount of flat surface area that can be imprinted using a G-clamp, and debossing larger areas requires a press capable of delivering literally tonnes of pressure, so a hand-debossed image will need to be kept quite small. The softer your surface, the deeper the debossing can be. The ideal surface is one with a little bit of give, but not too much, such as book cloth over grayboard.

Debossing dies are created commercially either from computer-generated artwork (text or line) or directly from clean, clear line drawings—the best results come from artwork with thinner, rather than fatter, lines or letters. The artwork is scanned photographically and output to film. This film is then used to transfer the image onto a metal plate, which is acid-etched to create the die. Importantly, the image is turned back to front during this process so that the resulting die will read backward, but will leave an impression that is the right way around.

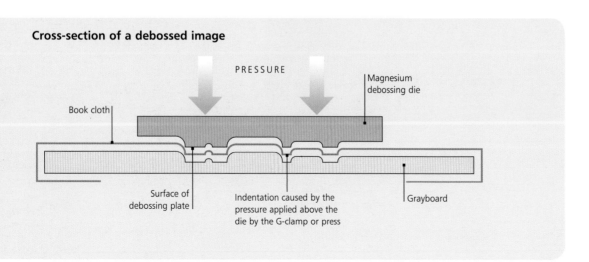

Cross-section of a debossed image

PRESSURE

Magnesium debossing die

Book cloth

Surface of debossing plate

Indentation caused by the pressure applied above the die by the G-clamp or press

Grayboard

Materials

- High-quality white paper or card for creating your artwork
- Case-bound cover, for example book cloth over grayboard

Tools

- Computer and printer, or black fibertip pen
- Blocking die, commissioned from your own design
- Cutting mat
- Solid table edge or board to clamp your work to
- G-clamp

CREATING A METAL DEBOSSING DIE

Debossing dies are produced professionally, and here you will learn how to create the right kind of artwork to commission a die.

Step 1
Consider the type of debossed impression you would like to make. Keep the design quite small, otherwise you will struggle to apply enough pressure to make any impression at all. The design could take the form of text, a pattern, or a crisp line drawing, either printed from a computer or drawn by hand. The artwork submitted should be black on a white background, and will produce a debossed impression exactly the same size. If printing from a computer, print with the highest resolution possible onto photo-quality paper stock.

ABOUT DIES
The dies used are known by several names, including blocking dies, foil blocking dies, metal stamps, foiling dies, photo-etched dies, hot stamp dies, and embossing dies. They can be made from magnesium, copper, steel, or brass, depending on the amount of detail required and the work the die will be required to do, and are produced in various gauges (thicknesses). Magnesium or steel dies of ¼ in. (6.4 mm) are suitable for the purposes described here.

Step 2
Locate a company that can produce a metal die for you—there are a number listed in the resources directory at the back of the book (see page 124). Send your flat, uncreased, "camera-ready" artwork with a letter requesting a ¼ in. (6.4 mm) magnesium stamping die, and state that "black will appear as debossed elements."

NOTE:
As the commissioning process varies from service to service it is crucial that you speak with your service provider before placing your order, to ensure you have described what you want correctly. Your die will usually take a few days to produce and its cost is dependent on its size—it is useful to get an indication of cost before going ahead with the order, to prevent any surprises.

DEBOSSING A COVER

In this example, the debossing process is carried out on the cover of a notebook.

Step 1

Place the book cover on a cutting mat on a flat surface near to the edge of a table or board. Place the die on top of the cover, exactly where you would like the impression to be made. Position your G-clamp so that it grips the die at the top and the table edge at the bottom, with the book cover sandwiched in the middle. Make sure the G-clamp is positioned centrally over the die—this is a matter of practice. Tighten the G-clamp as much as possible, until you feel a bit of give in the book cover.

Step 2

Undo the clamp and check that the impression has been made evenly, clearly, and to the required depth. If not, carefully fit the die back into the impression and position the G-clamp over the unfinished area(s). Often, the finished debossing can be achieved in one go, but occasionally you will need to clamp and reclamp a number of times.

NOTES:

• If your die is long and narrow rather than square, you may need to use two G-clamps at the same time, evenly spaced over the die.

• Depending on the shape of the die, exerting pressure on it may cause the die to bend and buckle slightly at the center. This is not a problem but will mean that once bent, it will be difficult to achieve a debossing without reclamping a number of times.

ALTERNATIVE MATERIALS

A range of alternative materials, such as leather, nubuck, and thick card, take debossings very well because of their firm but yielding surface.

Embossing

Embossing is a process by which a raised impression is made on the surface of the page by applying pressure using a two-piece embossing die.

While debossing (see page 88) is achieved simply by applying pressure through the die onto the surface, embossing traps the page between two separate die parts and molds the surface into a new shape. A "female" metal die is acid-etched with your design, then a "male" counterforce (or C-force) die, made of molten nylon, is contact-molded over the metal die. This results in the nylon being forced into the areas of the metal die that have been acid-etched, so creating the second part of the embossing die set. All of this is done commercially by the platemaker. If a sheet of paper is placed between these two die parts, and pressure applied, the surface of the paper will take on the exact molded shape of the acid-etched design—the nylon, male die forces the paper into the metal, female die.

When the embossing process is applied to a blank piece of paper the result will be a "blind" embossing, but it is possible to pre-print a design or text onto your sheet first and apply the embossing die by perfectly lining it up with the printed elements.

Here you will be shown how to commission an embossing die and hand emboss a design onto a page to create a piece of blind embossing.

DEFINING CHARACTERISTICS

Embossing uses a two-part die that is capable of producing quite precise areas of text or image raised above the surface of the page. The height of the raised mark depends on the depth of the acid-etching process applied to the female, metal die. The limits of the process are

dictated by the flexibility and ductility of your paper. If the etching of the die is too deep, the paper will split when you emboss with it. In addition, if the lines of your artwork are too thin, they will not translate properly.

Embossing (or embossing C-force) dies are created commercially either from computer-generated artwork (text or line) or directly from clean, clear line drawings. Your artwork is scanned photographically and output to film. This film is then used to transfer the image onto the metal die, which is then acid-etched to create the female die, from which the male is made. The metal die will appear back to front, but the nylon C-force will read correctly.

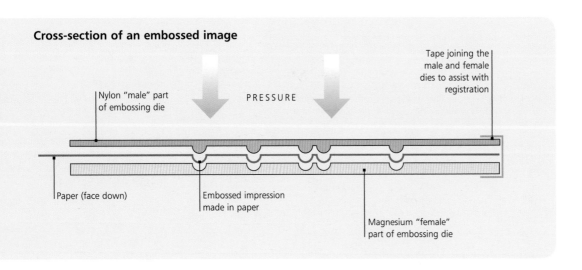

Cross-section of an embossed image

Nylon "male" part of embossing die

PRESSURE

Tape joining the male and female dies to assist with registration

Paper (face down)

Embossed impression made in paper

Magnesium "female" part of embossing die

Materials

- High-quality black paper or card for creating your artwork
- Paper for embossing: 75–80 lb (120–140 gsm), 8½ x 11 in. (21.5 x 28 cm)
- Adhesive tape
- Small piece of fabric, such as felt: 3 x 3 in. (8 x 8 cm)

Tools

- Computer and printer, or white fibertip pen
- Embossing die, commissioned from your own design
- Cutting mat
- Round-edged bone folder or flat-faced hammer (any object that can be used to apply flat, smooth pressure to the die surface)

CREATING AN EMBOSSING DIE

Embossing dies are produced professionally, and here you will learn how to create the right kind of artwork to commission your own die.

Step 1

Consider the type of embossing you would like to make on the surface of your work. It may be text, a pattern, or a crisp line drawing, either printed from a computer or drawn by hand. The artwork submitted should be white on a black background, and will produce an embossed impression exactly the same size. Ensure that your lines are not too fine, because very fine lines can lost in the etching process. If embossing onto thicker paper, your artwork will need thicker lines to cope. If printing from a computer, print with the highest resolution possible onto photo-quality paper stock. Wherever you place your embossing within the page, leave the same amount of blank space around your artwork as there is blank page between the embossing and the nearest edge of the sheet, and instruct your platemaker to trim the die accordingly. This is because the hand-embossing process requires one edge of the male and female plates to be in contact while embossing, otherwise it is impossible to line them up with each other.

ABOUT DIES

Embossing dies are usually made from magnesium and are available in various gauges (thicknesses). They are intended for use in a press, but here the application is improvised for hand embossing. Ideally a ¹⁄₁₆ in. (1.6 mm) female die should be used, although other thicknesses are suitable. The male die is then made directly from this female die.

Collection of embossing dies
Each embossing die has a two-part construction—the metal (female) part and the nylon (male) part. The female die is wrong-reading and the male die is right-reading.

NOTE:

As the commissioning process varies from service to service it is crucial that you speak with your service provider before placing your order, to ensure you have described what you want correctly. Your die will usually take a few days to produce and its cost is dependent on its size—it is useful to get an indication of cost before going ahead with the order to prevent any unpleasant surprises. Embossing dies are more expensive than debossing dies because there is an additional process to their production.

Distance from the edge of your die

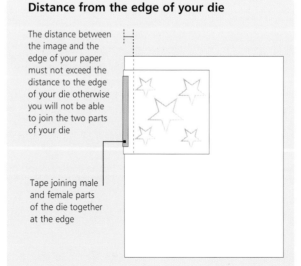

The distance between the image and the edge of your paper must not exceed the distance to the edge of your die otherwise you will not be able to join the two parts of your die

Tape joining male and female parts of the die together at the edge

Step 2

Locate a company that can produce a metal die for you—there are a number listed in the resources directory at the back of the book (see page 124). Send your flat, uncreased, "camera-ready" artwork with a letter requesting a ¹⁄₁₆ in. (1.6 mm) magnesium C-force embossing die, and state that "white will appear as embossed elements." State that you are using it for embossing (raised work) and not debossing.

EMBOSSING A PAGE

Step 1

Attach the C-force (nylon) part of the die to the metal part along one edge, using adhesive tape. The edge that you choose will depend on the position of your embossing on the final sheet, and consequently which edges of the die need to remain open and accessible. Once attached, place the metal part of the die on a flat surface. Carefully slip your sheet of paper face down between the two parts of the die and check that the parts are aligned—this can only be done if one of the sides is taped, as described, to act as a hinge and registration point.

Step 2

Once you are confident that the two parts of the die are aligned, use a round-edged bone folder or flat-faced hammer to carefully rub over the areas where your design occurs, supporting the rest of the die with your other hand to prevent it from moving. It helps to apply this pressure through a small piece of fabric, such as felt, to even out and soften the impact of the tool face on the plastic. The embossing is created by pushing the paper down into the metal die.

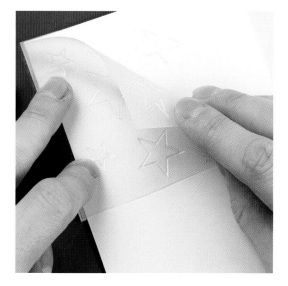

Step 3

Lift up the nylon part to check your progress, then precisely reposition the paper and nylon before reapplying pressure. You may need to go over the embossed areas more than once to get an even, crisp result.

VARIATION

It is possible to achieve an embossed or debossed effect using cutout shapes and letters rather than dies—for *Turn Over Darling* (see page 111), Ron King embossed his image using fine rope. Here, cutout shapes are embossed into a sheet of damp watercolor paper.

You will need:

- Watercolor paper
- Felt, same size as watercolor paper
- Two pressing boards
- Plastic wrap
- Cutout shapes

Place a piece of felt over a pressing board, then place your dampened watercolor sheet over the felt. Cover with a sheet of plastic wrap, then place your cutout shape on top. Finally, place a second pressing board on top and apply as much pressure as possible—this can be achieved using G-clamps, your own body weight, or an etching or nipping press. Keep in position for five minutes, then dry flat, but not below a heavy weight.

This method will create a debossed effect on the top surface of the sheet and an embossed effect on the reverse, so if you are using cut letters, consider their orientation according to the effect you want—letters and words will need to be turned back to front if you want to achieve embossed text.

Folding the page

Folding can bring a third dimension to the page, and with it the play of light and shadow that the flat page alone cannot achieve.

Folding is absolutely integral to the construction of most books and bindings, but usually takes on a supporting role, creating the spine or allowing the reader to turn from one page to the next. To bring folding into the foreground and make a decorative or sculptural feature of it requires a very different approach. No longer just a functional element of the book, the decorative fold allows you to transform the page into a visual playground where light and shade become your paint.

The first examples of origami, meaning "folded paper" in Japanese, can be traced back to the sixth century, when paper first arrived in Japan as a cultural export from nearby China. It is not known whether the European development of paper folding developed directly from the Japanese art, or whether it had an entirely independent development.

Paper folding within the book form has borrowed a little from the traditions of origami, but, due to the constraints of the bound page, bookmakers have often chosen folding techniques that bring a whole new dimension to the page and the journey through the book. Working in tandem with the book's form, some use the fold to hide and reveal parts of their narrative that only the reader has the privilege of discovering. Others use new and innovative folding techniques to create labyrinthine sculptural forms whose primary design is to play with light and form. Here you will be shown how to create a sculptural book based entirely on a single folded sheet, using a pattern of scores and folds characteristic of its shape.

DEFINING CHARACTERISTICS

There are practical and aesthetic considerations involved with the use of folding in a book project. The first consideration is grain. Folding is always easier with the grain, rather than against it, but it is not always possible to conform to this rule if you are attempting to push the boundaries beyond conventional folding. Where this is not possible, scoring your crease mark before folding will help you achieve clean, crisp fold lines. The weight of your paper is also a fundamental consideration. Folding is more straightforward with lightweight paper, and as soon as you go beyond about 80 lb (140 gsm) it becomes more difficult and less accurate. Again, marking and scoring before you fold will help you to achieve a clean fold. You will never achieve a flat fold with heavier paper because every fold has a spring-loading— an energy trapped in the fold that needs the weight of a cover or other pages to keep it contained. Finally, remember that every fold has two sides, or faces, that play differently with the light, lending a dynamic element to any folded book that will respond beautifully to interaction and movement.

Materials

- **Sheet for folding:** one sheet 80 lb (140 gsm) paper, 3½ x 39 in. (9 x 99 cm)
- **Grayboard:** two circular pieces, 4 in. (10 cm) diameter
- **Cover paper:** two circular pieces, 5 in. (13 cm) diameter
- **Scrap paper**
- **PVA/paste mix**
- **Endpapers:** two circular pieces 90 lb (180 gsm) paper, of 3½ in. (9 cm) diameter
- **Glue stick**

Tools

- Pencil
- Ruler
- Bone folder
- Scalpel and cutting mat
- Glue brush
- Book weight or heavy, flat object

CREATING SPIRAL-FOLD PAGES

The following simple folding technique creates a surprisingly elegant end result. Just follow the marking and scoring instructions, which can be varied in size and angle to create different extremes of the same form.

Step 1
Take your sheet of paper and use a pencil to mark the scoring points as follows: along one long edge place a mark at 1 in. (2.5 cm), then ½ in. (1 cm) further on, then 1 in. (2.5 cm) further on, then ½ in. (1 cm) further on, and so on all the way along the edge.

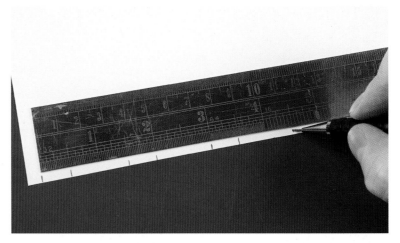

Step 2
On the unmarked long edge (and with the marked edge still at the top), make a mark at ¼ in. (0.75 cm) in from the left. This is the point at which you can begin marking the score marks for your lower edge. This time begin with the ½ in. (1 cm) measurement then mark 1 in. (2.5 cm) beyond this, and alternate all the way along the edge, as before.

Step 3
Once all the points are marked, use the point of a bone folder to carefully score a line between the first mark on the bottom line and the top left-hand corner of the page. Then score between the next mark on the bottom line and the first mark on the top line, and so on along the sheet.

Step 4
Carefully fold along each score line, alternating the direction of the fold each time, first folding forward and then backward with each subsequent score line. Once you have completed the folding, trim off the incomplete folds that are left over at each end.

MAKING A COVER

This type of fold transforms a long sheet of paper into a spiral concertina, so you will need to make a circular cover for it. This will not only protect the pages, but will act to contain and flatten the energy held within the folds.

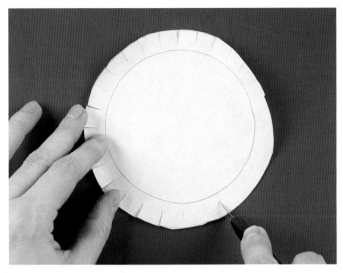

Step 1
Place a grayboard circle centrally on the reverse of a cover paper circle and draw around it with a pencil. Then make slits all around the circumference of the cover piece, about ⅛ in. (3 mm) away from the drawn line, out to the edge. Make these marks approximately every ½ in. (12 mm). Repeat for the second cover.

Step 2
With scrap paper under your work, carefully glue out your cover paper with PVA/paste mix, ensuring that you glue right to the edge. Place a grayboard circle in the center and turn down each flap of cover paper, one by one, so that the grayboard is enclosed all the way around. Check that the edge is as smooth as possible, and leave to dry under a flat weight. Do the same for the second cover.

Step 3
Glue your endpapers down centrally onto each cover. Then, with a glue stick, glue out one end fold of your concertina and position it centrally on your endpaper. Before firming it in place, check that the whole concertina is central, and adjust if not. Repeat this for the other end of the concertina, this time ensuring that the two covers are positioned in line with each other before firming down. Dry under a flat weight.

Pop-up

Pop-up is one of the most intriguing and attractive ways to alter the page and typically involves transforming the flat, two-dimensional sheet into a three-dimensional stage using cuts, folds, and add-ons.

The term "pop-up" refers to a range of methods of making three-dimensional space from a two-dimensional sheet. This special transformation is constructed in such a way that it can be activated simply by the reader opening the page, or by the use of flaps and tabs that the reader pulls or pushes to enact a physical change in the page. Pop-up techniques include complex cuts and folds within a single sheet, or the addition of glued-in paper and card to create scenes, but common to all is the dynamic transformation of the page in the hands of the reader.

The long history of pop-up began in the thirteenth and fourteenth centuries, and was initially used as an educational tool within books on subjects such as anatomy and physiology. It wasn't until the end of the eighteenth century, with advances in printing techniques, that pop-up books and cards began to be produced for entertainment, particularly for children. Victorian Britain was the epicenter of this development until techniques spread across Europe and were once again pushed forward by advances in printing and manufacturing techniques, particularly in Germany. Pop-up and paper-engineering techniques eventually traveled full-circle back to their roots in educational books.

Pop-up designers working today, such as Robert Sabuda, create highly elaborate three-dimensional scenes that efficiently and magically transform the page like a butterfly emerging from a chrysalis. Here the focus will be on a pop-up technique called the parallel fold, which involves cuts and folds that create the illusion of three-dimensional space on the page. No additional material is glued or fixed in. This kind of pop-up is ideal for incorporating into concertina books.

DEFINING CHARACTERISTICS

Pop-ups are essentially about interactive, dynamic changes that take place within a single spread. They are about bringing the book to life by engaging the reader in transformative processes that they are required to be a part of; they enact the narrative by turning the page, pulling a tab, or lifting a flap. The process brings into sharp focus the idea that the book is dormant until opened up, and that it is dependent on the reader to bring it to life. This is, of course, true of all books, but pop-up takes this notion and breathes physical life into it.

Techniques and mechanisms often involve the addition of glued paper elements to the existing page that either move, change, or reveal information when interacted with. Likewise, when the book is closed these elements once again revert to their original position. Pop-ups require an enormous amount of planning and experimentation, and are perhaps the most complex page treatments that the bookmaker can attempt.

The most basic characteristic of a pop-up is that the act of the page-turn itself provides the moment of transformation, whether this is achieved by gluing elements to one or both pages, or cutting and folding into the page. It is movement itself that is the essence and magic of the pop-up.

Materials

+ Sheet for the pop-up:
  one sheet 80 lb
  (140 gsm) white paper,
  8½ x 11 in.
  (21 x 29 cm or A4),
  for photocopying onto

Tools

+ Scalpel, steel ruler,
  and cutting mat
+ Bone folder

CREATING A POP-UP

In order to help you understand how cut-and-fold pop-ups are constructed, templates for three different pop-ups have been printed opposite. Every cut-and-fold pop-up is constructed of cut lines, and two types of fold lines: fold and reverse fold.

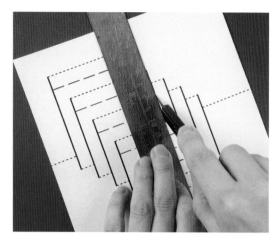

Step 1

Photocopy your chosen pop-up template—template A is the simplest to construct, while C is the most difficult. If possible, ensure that the grain of your photocopy paper runs parallel with the dotted fold lines on the template, and adjust your image orientation accordingly. This is especially important if you are photocopying onto heavier paper. Each solid line requires cutting with a scalpel. The short-dotted lines represent folds that are in the same direction as the fold of the page, while the long-dotted lines represent reverse folds—folds that go in the opposite direction to the page fold. Begin by cutting the solid lines carefully with a scalpel and steel rule.

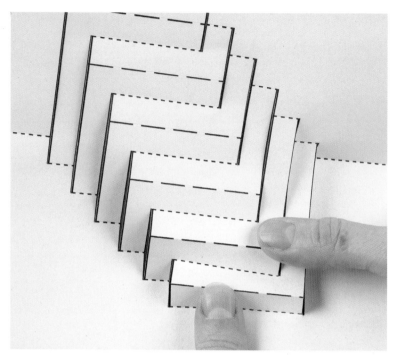

Step 2

Carefully score each fold line with the point of a bone folder or similar tool—a ballpoint pen that has run out of ink is great for the job. Scoring the lines will assist you in the folding process, which can be very fiddly. Once scored, fold the main page-fold line. Next, fold the short-dotted line folds in the same direction as the main page fold.

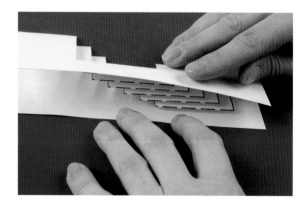

Step 3

Now fold all of the long-dotted lines in the opposite direction. Once all of these have been folded, you should be able to carefully fold down the whole, as if closing a book. The pop-up should sit flat in a closed book, and re-open perfectly.

NOTE:

To avoid visible printed lines appearing on the front of your pop-up, photocopy the plan on a faint photocopier setting, then fold all lines in the opposite direction to that indicated by the template, so that the pop-up is on the reverse of the sheet where no lines are printed. This can even be done once you have completed all the above steps. However, it also means that your pop-up is in mirror image. Alternatively, simply copy the flat plan in pencil, then rub out your pencil lines once your pop-up is constructed.

Double parallel fold (A)

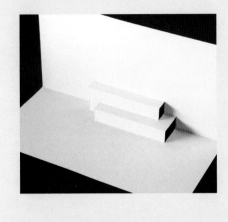

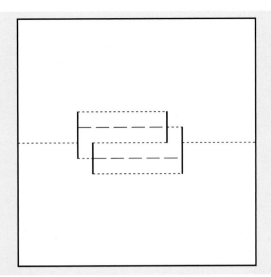

Stairs (B)

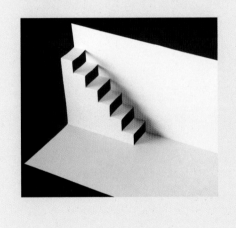

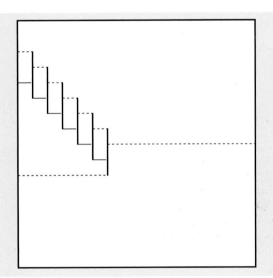

Complex stairs (C)

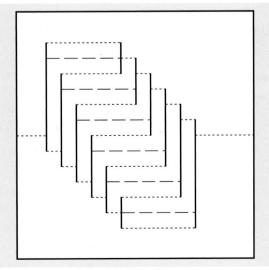

Books communicate with us in visual, tactile, imaginative, and intellectual ways. Sometimes we are aware of how a book communicates, and at other times they do so subtly and unconsciously. Understanding how books convey their magic and the enormous range of communicative methods available to the bookmaker is fundamental to the creation of interesting and engaging books, whether they are notebooks, scrapbooks, or complex pieces of book art.

Books are fundamentally about imaginative space, whether that of the writer or the reader. They provide a blank canvas for ideas and stories, and create private worlds unrivaled by many other media.

The books in this chapter have been chosen to highlight the potential of the techniques outlined in the rest of the book, and to show the possibilities open to those with a good basic set of binding skills. Almost all of the examples use techniques and formats achievable by hand. Where that is not the case, artists have improvised and invented bindings that solve particular problems, whether these solutions are functional, decorative, or conceptual in nature. As you gain confidence as a bookmaker and decide which rules work for you and which can be broken, the book form will become a vehicle for rich experimentation and creativity.

CHAPTER THREE:
the complete book

Structure and narrative

The structure of a book can be thought of as the method by which the pages are bound, and how they relate physically to each other as the book is read and handled. The narrative is the journey within the book that the author or maker leads the reader through, and may be visual, textual, or a combination of the two. The books in this section use manipulations of structure to get their message across in an innovative way.

BOOK ONE

Dos-à-dos
BOUND TO ARGUE BY HEATHER WESTON

This notebook employs a dos-à-dos structure, chosen to fit perfectly with its theme. It is a notebook designed for writing in, but because of the specific structure it utilizes, two books are created within one cover. Its title, *Bound to Argue*, hints at this structural play, because the two books face in opposite directions, perhaps ready to accommodate the opposing or contradictory opinions of its owner.

MATERIALS AND TECHNIQUES
Two seven-leaf single-section books are stapled either side of one continuous cover that runs from back to front. The text is printed on both sides of the cover, while the inner pages remain blank. Because of the nature of the structure, the text that begins on the inside of the cover ends on the outside, and vice-versa. The book was stapled using an electric saddle stapler. This handmade notebook was assembled in small batches.

The dos-à-dos structure allows for two books within one

Each single-section book is stapled separately into the folded cover

The cover is one continuous piece that runs from front to back

The book's title, *Bound To Argue*, runs from inside to out and from back to front

The subtitle, *every argument has a flip side*, runs on the inside, from front to back

BOOK TWO

Concertina variant
12.38–14.16 BY DANIELA DEEG AND CYNTHIA LOLLIS, ETC. PRESS

This book visually documents a journey made by the two artists, beginning at New York Public Library and ending in Battery Park at the southern tip of Manhattan. Every seven minutes they paused to photograph the view down the center of the street, documenting that particular moment in their journey. This was then repeated in the opposite direction for their return.

The book itself is a seven-spread double concertina that can enclose itself to create a double-walled star. On the outside face of the concertina sit the seven views created during their punctuated outward journey. On the inside are the images captured on the return. The exterior of the book thus represents an impression of where they were traveling to, and the interior where they had already been.

MATERIALS AND TECHNIQUES
The two screen-printed concertinas are bound together at each of the seven points and the ensemble is bound into Plexiglas covers.

The whole book comes in a grayboard box and was produced in a limited edition of 36.

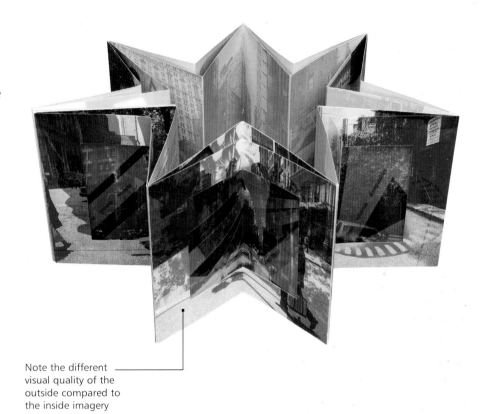

Note the different visual quality of the outside compared to the inside imagery

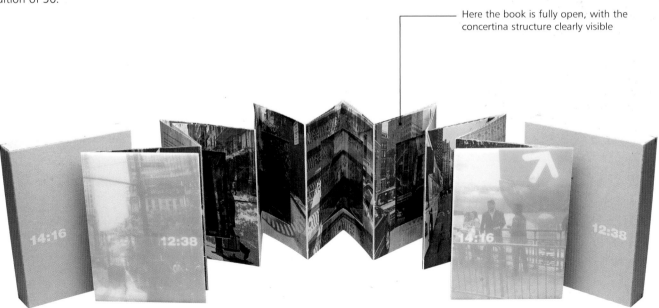

Here the book is fully open, with the concertina structure clearly visible

Structure as metaphor
DOLLY: EDITION UNLIMITED BY KAREN BLEITZ

Dolly is a piece of book art that explores the subject of animal cloning, exploiting the very nature of the book's repeating page structure and utilizing it as a metaphor for the reproduction of genetically identical animals. Each of the 45 pages represents a separate but identical animal, the only difference between them being the order in which they appear within the sequence. Text taken from scientific articles is reproduced in letterpress print on the cover of the book, but the sheep-shaped pages themselves are blank and voiceless.

The book is sewn at the spine and the sheep jigsaw-cut by hand at exactly the right point to incorporate the binding at the rump; the binding perhaps representing the element that links them all—the original genetic material. The sheep shape can be popped out of the main book structure that houses it and opens up fully to reveal the 45-page free-standing flock of cloned animals, all identically sized and shaped.

MATERIALS AND TECHNIQUES

An adapted two-hole sewing technique was used to hand bind the single pages into the spine. The book block was then sandwiched and glued between two cover boards. The shape of the sheep was traced onto the outside of the board at exactly the right position to incorporate the binding into Dolly's rump. Dolly was then hand-cut using a jigsaw.

Dolly was planned in an edition size of 17, but because of the precision needed in the jigsawing phase, three were lost during production, an occupational hazard when employing complex bindings.

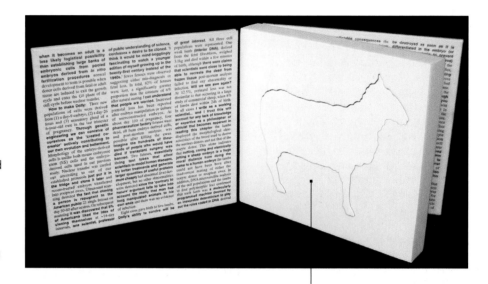

The single, voiceless sheep, surrounded by scientific text, waits to be liberated from the constraints of her biology

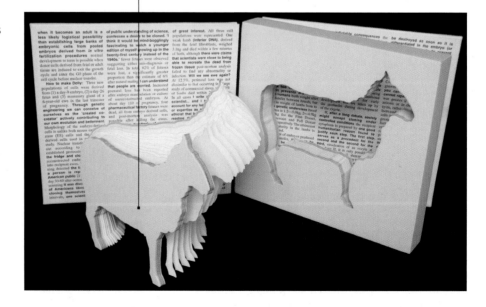

Dolly is released from her confines, and can be opened up to reveal that she is in fact a whole flock of clones

Hybrid structure
INFINITY BOOK **BY ANNE RIZK**

Infinity Book was designed as a blank binding to house material divided into two distinct sections. It takes as its starting point the concertina-fold page, but instead of simply binding this into two cover boards, two concertinas are cleverly bound at one end by single cover boards and at the other end into the two inside covers of a case-bound shell. The advantage of this innovative binding is that it allows the contents to be compartmentalized and divided, but, at the same time, folds neatly around a single cover for efficient storage and handling.

MATERIALS AND TECHNIQUES
The cover is made of silk book cloth bound over board with separate matching end covers. The concertina-folded paper could be any stock or color, but would particularly suit a heavy, watercolor-quality sheet contrasting with the cover color.

This book was initially produced as a prototype to demonstrate to clients, and has since been used as a format for many commissions.

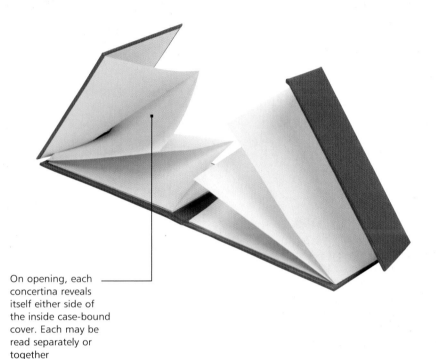

On opening, each concertina reveals itself either side of the inside case-bound cover. Each may be read separately or together

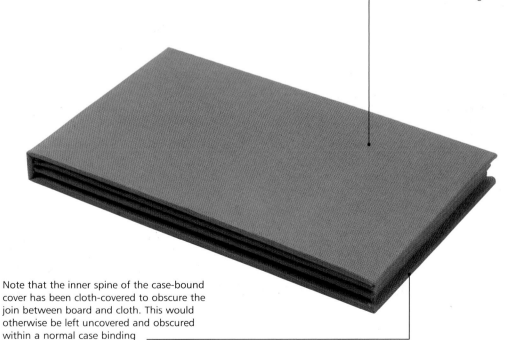

Folded closed, the book neatly conceals its butterfly-like nature, with hard-bound covers resembling a normal book

Note that the inner spine of the case-bound cover has been cloth-covered to obscure the join between board and cloth. This would otherwise be left uncovered and obscured within a normal case binding

Concertina with a twist
A DICTION BY HEATHER WESTON

Although *A Diction* utilizes a basic concertina structure with cloth-bound covers, the usual rectangular shape of the page has been replaced with a tapered shape similar to that of a beer glass, where the top is wider than the bottom. This design not only mirrors its subject matter, alcohol addiction, but also enables the concertina to form a full circle when opened completely, with front cover meeting back cover. The text that forms the narrative within the book reflects this circle, or cycle, of addiction, and like addiction itself, flows around and around, seemingly without end.

MATERIALS AND TECHNIQUES

This is a 36-page, hand-folded concertina book with a tapered page shape. One large sheet was printed offset lithography using QuarkXPress layout software, then cut down into four arcs, before hand-scoring and folding. It uses Gmund Bier, a commercial paper made from recycled beer labels, hops, and malt. It has a cloth-bound cover with a blind debossed title on the front and a pint motif debossing on the reverse.

A Diction was printed in a run of 150 and was hand-assembled to order.

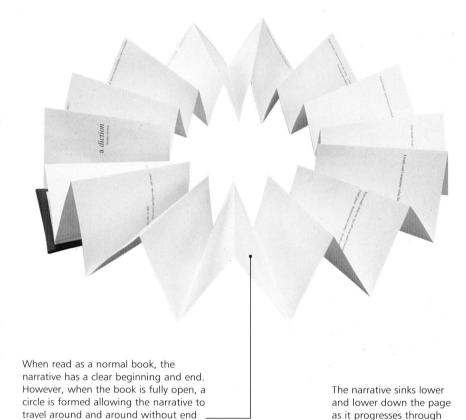

When read as a normal book, the narrative has a clear beginning and end. However, when the book is fully open, a circle is formed allowing the narrative to travel around and around without end

The narrative sinks lower and lower down the page as it progresses through the book, as if mimicking the liquid in a glass

The standard concertina with a twist—note the tapered page shape that defines the way the book unfolds on a curve

Surface, light, and shadow

The pages of books live in the dark. Only on opening do we cast light over their surface and render them readable. The surface of the paper itself brings depth to the page and texture to the fingertips. The books within this section use light, shade, and surface to full effect, encompassing a combination of cutting, embossing, and layering.

BOOK SIX

Embossing or debossing?
TURN OVER DARLING BY RON KING

This beautifully efficient piece of book art uses a simple embossed graphic element to explore the turning of the page. An embossed image on one side of the sheet becomes a debossed image on its reverse.

The book is made up of six full-page images that, when bound at the center, create eleven separate nudes in the sequence. As each page is turned, the embossed lines on the recto become the debossed lines on the verso, lending themselves first to one image, then in turn to the next in the sequence.

The title cleverly alludes both to the dynamic process of the turning of the page and to the book's subject matter.

MATERIALS AND TECHNIQUES
Using heavy pressure, shaped wire was pressed into damp sheets of khadi paper to create the deeply embossed/debossed line drawings, then the wire was removed and the sheets left to dry on a rack. The six sheets were then folded and lightly bound with a thread that wraps around the whole book and its cover. The artist wanted to avoid a binding that required punching holes in the sheets, but also wanted the reader to be able to unbind the book and view the pages as spreads.

This book was produced as an unlimited, numbered edition.

Deep embossing is created using wire on damp paper

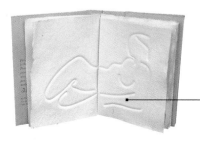

The embossed image on one page transforms into the debossed image of the subsequent page

BOOK SEVEN

The hand-cut page
BOY MEETS GIRL **BY METTE AMBECK**

Boy Meets Girl combines considerations of structure, surface, and sequence to delight the reader with a subtle and silent narrative. Beginning from one end of the book, the "boy" is cut out of the page, and progressively more of him is revealed with each subsequent page. From the other end of the book the "girl" is cut, and again, more and more is cut and revealed with each page. It is not until you get to the center of the book that boy actually comes face to face with girl. The eye area is the first to be cut out in both cases and, without realizing it at the start, it becomes clear that they have had their eye on each other right from the beginning.

MATERIALS AND TECHNIQUES

This book uses cuts alone to deliver its narrative—there is no ink and no color on the page. Each page was painstakingly hand cut, with only a line template as guidance. The book was then bound using a multi-section method, with an eight-hole stitch. It was then case-bound in a silver cover.

Boy Meets Girl was produced in an edition of five.

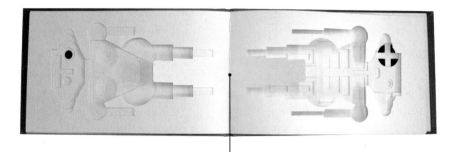

It is not until the center of the book that boy comes face to face with girl

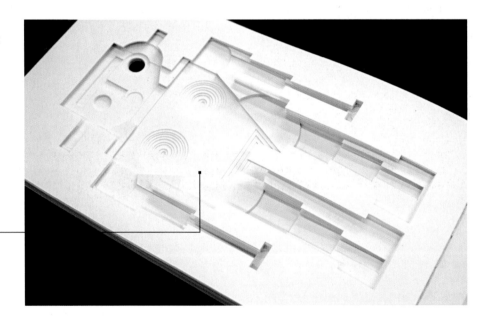

Each page is carefully cut by hand with a scalpel

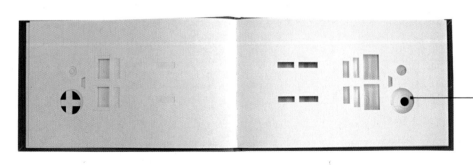

Two or three pages in from the front it is not yet clear what the reader is looking at, with only the eye area cut out

Layer upon layer
BLUE TO BLUE BY KATSUMI KOMAGATA

Blue to Blue is a beautifully crafted children's story inspired by the author's memory of swimming in the sea for the first time as a small boy, and noticing the merging boundaries between sea and sky. Written in Japanese, the book tells the story of the lifecycle of young salmon, whose journey from egg to adulthood takes them far and wide and, eventually, back to their place of birth. Komagata uses a delicate sequence of die-cut pages to explore the shapes and textures of this journey and its characters, employing a vast array of Japanese papers in the process.

MATERIALS AND TECHNIQUES
Although now commercially produced in large numbers, the book was initially designed and prototyped by hand, allowing the author to experiment widely with sequencing and cut-throughs. The binding is a variant of perfect binding, with the addition of a stitch down the length of the book prior to attaching the cover. The pages and cover were die-cut, trimmed, and assembled mechanically, although most of this could be achieved by hand.

The book has been reprinted 12 times, each time with a print run of 2,800.

Each layer uses the subsequent layer as a backdrop, adding depth and variety to every phase of the story

The cover hints at the layering below via a die-cut hole

BOOK NINE

Blind embossing
BORGES AND I BY HEATHER WESTON

Jorge Luis Borges wrote *Borges and I* during the time that he was losing his sight. The text documents a battle of wills between the invincible writer and the mortal man. To bring this battle to life in her book, the artist has used blind embossing to convey a secondary text that reads as an entirely new text within the original. The main text is represented by black print and the secondary by blind-embossed text. Both are on a black background, the subtext of blindness being firmly brought to the reader's attention—the book must be read in a good light.

MATERIALS AND TECHNIQUES
The black text was printed onto black paper using offset lithography, four-to-a-page, leaving gaps where the blind-embossed text was to be placed. The pages were then cut and folded into their six-page concertinas. The embossing was achieved by hand using embossing plates. Endpapers were attached and the completed book was bound into two cloth-bound covers.

The book was printed in a run of 120, then made to order.

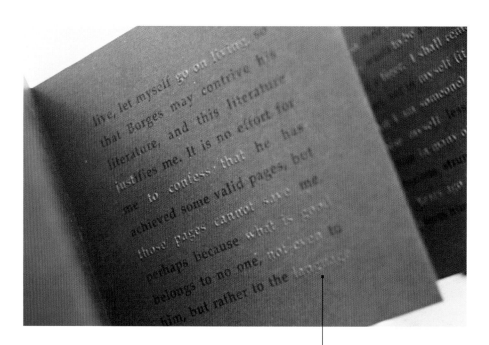

The book follows a basic concertina model and uses only the front face of the concertina

Blind-embossed text stands proud of the surface of the page and can be read as a separate text, in addition to the text as a whole

Cut and fold
THE JANTE LAW BY METTE AMBECK

BOOK
TEN

The Jante Law is a set of ten commandments or rules that are said to reveal how Danish identity is dogged by inferiority and inadequacy. Although fictional, the power of these commandments is known throughout Denmark and beyond. Mette Ambeck's re-presentation of these rules within her book is an attempt to symbolically and physically break up the rigidity and conformity laid down within the commandments, and present a reconfigured, freer, more creative relationship to them. The restraining dimension of the book is cut into, broken up, and reassembled—the end result of which is a book so unique and arresting that it defies not only the Jante rules, but also the rules of what constitutes a book.

MATERIALS AND TECHNIQUES
The basic, standard page has been mathematically broken down into square-based strips. These strips, all containing ten pages, were then reconstituted to make the book. There are 100 small pages in all, and each was concertina folded, hand-cut, and attached to the next with glue. When the book is opened, these pages behave, to a certain extent, like the pages of a pop-up book, but also have the effect of restraining the act of opening.

The cover is bound in buckram and the title was sculpted onto the cover as if embossed.

This book was produced in an edition of ten.

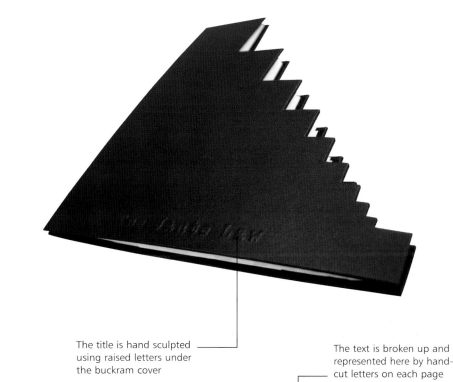

The title is hand sculpted using raised letters under the buckram cover

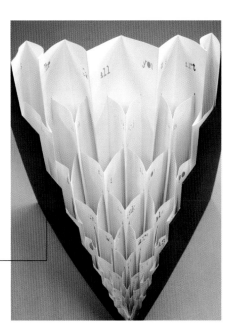

The cover has a stepped edge representing the ten Jante rules, and the "pages" are fixed within its frame

The text is broken up and represented here by hand-cut letters on each page

Transformations

Some books are more transformative than others, containing hidden dimensions that need to be discovered and unleashed by the reader, and revealing metamorphoses of shape, size, and depth. The books in the following section use dynamic and economical ways of transforming their narrative and structure to become more than meets the eye.

BOOK ELEVEN

Sheet or book?
***THE BOOKMAKER* BY DEB RINDL**

At first sight, *The Bookmaker* appears to be a small folded and printed book-like object housed in a box. However, as the hands explore and expose its workings, and the eye takes in its fragmented and almost decorative text, the reader comes to discover that it is constructed from a single sheet of paper. As the sheet reveals itself, the text, no longer fragmented, conveys instructions for making a book from a single sheet of paper. The metamorphosis between raw and finished state betrays the simplicity of its structure. On the one hand it is a book, on the other a sheet, the transformation being enacted via cuts and folds. This is, after all, the very essence of bookmaking.

MATERIALS AND TECHNIQUES
The book was printed in two colors using offset lithography. The cuts and folds were then applied by hand, following a specific pattern. The artist sees this finishing process as an essential part of reclaiming the book as a handmade object.

The book was produced in an edition of 150.

Exploring the book reveals a meandering, concertina fold with printed text on both sides

First impressions are of a small, multi-page book

When fully open the book reveals its origins—a single flat sheet

Flag book
DESTINATION MOON BY KAREN HANMER

Karen Hanmer has worked with the flag book structure on a number of occasions, because of its capacity to accommodate more than one visual or textual narrative at once. With any flag book, there is a transformative moment at the point when the covers are pulled apart, where the sequential reading of the book suddenly and dynamically transforms into the panoramic. Hanmer uses this dynamic tension as a fitting metaphor to launch this book's narratives about space travel. Its two texts are presented in the sequential reading, along with the imagery, but are hidden when the book is viewed panoramically. The moment of transformation is, of course, accompanied by the characteristic "swoosh" of the flag book's pages, which seems particularly fitting for this subject matter.

MATERIALS AND TECHNIQUES
Destination Moon uses a Hedi Kyle's flag book structure, in this case seven pages across and three deep. The book was printed using an inkjet printer—the cover and spine used uncoated paper, whereas the image and text pages used a coated paper. The book was produced in an edition of 20.

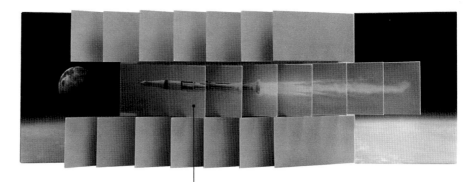

When the book is fully open, the complete 21-page panorama is visible

The sequential view of the book allows it to be read as a traditional book would be

The covers and spine are illustrated with a striking moonscape

BOOK THIRTEEN

Book as theater
TUNNEL VISION BY MARIA G. PISANO, MEMORY PRESS © 2004

Maria's book uses the tunnel format to present the artist's creative exploration of the Holland Tunnel, connecting New York with New Jersey. Scenes of a magical underwater world shared by both cars and fish are presented on the inside of the eight-stage book, while the story of the artist coming to America and historical facts about the tunnel, its engineer, and workers are printed on the outside concertina support. The exterior of the book has a tiled pattern, making reference to the six million tiles that were used to line the tunnel.

When closed and flat, this book withholds its theatrical secrets. By contrast, open it up and you are lured into a three-dimensional world large enough to allow an almost physical exploration of its space: when fully extended the book reaches 6½ ft (2 m) in length.

MATERIALS AND TECHNIQUES
The artist uses quite an array of image-making techniques, including intaglio, chine-collé, relief, lithography, and digital printing, giving a rich and varied visual language to the book's surface. There are eight cut, vertical panels, flanked characteristically by a concertina at each side, forming the walls of the tunnel. As befitting a tunnel, there is an entrance and exit to the book, at back and front.

Tunnel Vision was produced in an edition of 25.

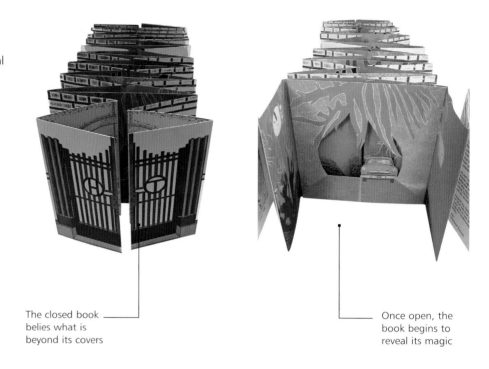

The closed book belies what is beyond its covers

Once open, the book begins to reveal its magic

The viewer is drawn into the eight-panel tunnel

Creative carousel
NEW YORK DREAMS BY ANDREA DEZSÖ

This book emerged out of a very particular experience. The artist had traveled to New York from Hungary and was to stay there for a year as an artist in residence. However, her baby son remained behind in Budapest. The book documents that emotional time, with images of New York interlaced with powerful imagery from dreams and memories of her son. The book is a classic five-scene carousel, but its intricately hand-decorated pages deliver a depth and intensity in line with its complex, multilayered narrative.

MATERIALS AND TECHNIQUES
Pages made from handmade watercolor rag paper were stitched together with black, waxed string. The cover cloth is dark blue silk with an inlay for a small hand-painted label, and the book can be tied together in a carousel shape with a black silk ribbon. The imagery was produced using watercolors, acrylics, inks, and colored pencils.

This book is one of a kind.

The closed carousel waits to be brought to life

All five scenes can be viewed when the concertina is fully open

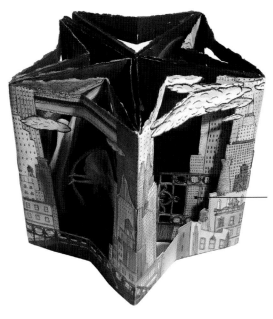

Once tied open, the multilayered scenes are exposed in all their depth and richness

Pushing the boundaries

Many bookmakers challenge themselves to push the format to its extremes. This section features a small collection of works that do just that. Perhaps it could be argued that they can no longer be called books, but the visual and structural language that they employ is so fundamentally "bookish" that their origins are clear.

BOOK FIFTEEN
Book or sculpture?
A SECRET HELIOTROPISM BY NICOLA DALE

Nicola Dale's *A Secret Heliotropism* takes as its starting point an existing book—*The People's History*, a populist twentieth-century history book—and transforms it beyond recognition. At the core of this work is an examination of Walter Benjamin's thesis on the philosophy of history, in which he makes the analogy between the heliotropism of plants—their natural inclination toward the sun—and the subjectivity of our view of historical events, ever-dependent on our moral, temporal, or geographical viewpoint. Every page within this 320-page book is hand cut, transforming each from its predictable, fixed position into a collection of highly malleable and movable leaf strands, mirroring Benjamin's thesis. When not on show, the leaves can be gathered and folded down flat and the cover closed, returning the book to its more recognizable form.

MATERIALS AND TECHNIQUES
The book took a year to complete, reflecting not only the precision of the cutting process but also, by good fortune, one cycle of the Earth's movement around the sun. An intricate stencil was drawn onto each page. The pages were then cut, one by one, using a scalpel. Although the template was the same for each page, every page is unique, due to the nature of hand-cutting. This book is one of a kind, for obvious reasons.

Each page can be folded flat, the cover closed, and the leaves deprived of their light once again

Each page is cut and transformed from flat leaf to searching tendril

BOOK SIXTEEN

Materials and form
VESSELS BY ADELE OUTTERIDGE

Vessels explores the idea of the book as container, not of information but of space, rhythm, and form. The artist uses *Vessels* to explore the book form in its own right, without any need for function or content in the traditional sense. The use of transparent pages allows the book to be read in one glance, with all its working elements visible, and their structural function clear. The resulting object is a rather ethereal and sculptural creature, seemingly far removed from its pedestrian, bookish origins.

MATERIALS AND TECHNIQUES
Vessels is composed of thirty-two Perspex pages bound together at the spine with twine using a Coptic, single-sheet binding developed by the artist. The three "vessels" within the book are created using white, gray, and black linen threads, fed through the pages via small, drilled holes. These connect each page to the next, but more importantly, create the visual vessels within the book.

An edition of ten is in production.

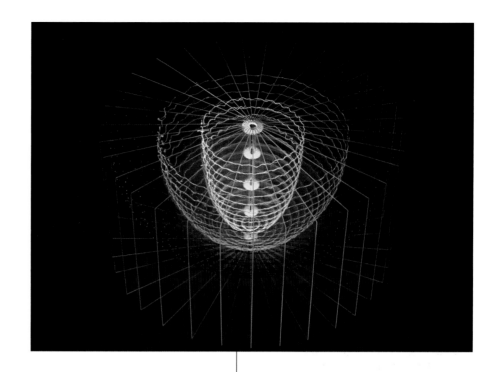

The use of Perspex enables the reader to view all the pages at once, and see how they are joined together

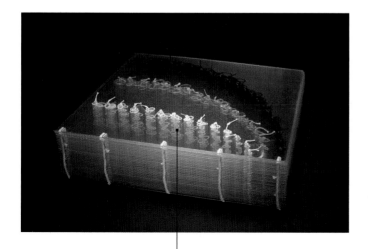

The closed object looks reassuringly book-like

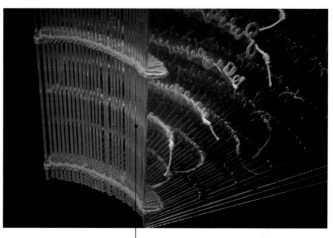

The close-up reveals not only the spine binding, but also how each page is joined to the next through holes in the Perspex

Is it still a book?
BLUE DIP NECKLACE BY RACHEL HAZELL

Inspired by the icescapes of Antarctica, *Blue Dip Necklace* sits on the edge of "bookness." Its methods of construction are certainly from a bookbinding tradition, yet the finished object, looking more like a medieval ruff, transcends the book's limitations. The intention of the maker was to subvert the form and test what may be defined in book terms, but at the same time to adhere solidly to bookmaking methods. The end result is a beautiful object, neither book nor necklace, but something that can stand on its own, straddling the two forms.

MATERIALS AND TECHNIQUES
The book is constructed of small, heavyweight paper pages, all sewn together with a continuous kettle stitch at top and bottom. The pages were dipped into blue watercolor resulting in each page taking up the ink differently.

   This book is one of a kind.

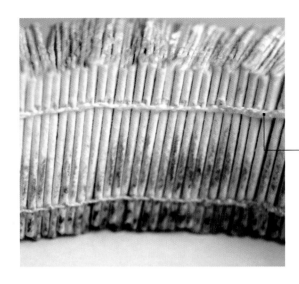

A close-up shows the kettle stitch that runs around the center of the whole object, binding the pages.

Book or necklace?

BOOK EIGHTEEN

Reflective surfaces
LE 6 AVRIL 1944 BY JACQUES FOURNIER, ROSELIN EDITIONS

Although a large departure from the book form, there are many features of this object that use book-like methods, including its material, its use of text, and the juxtaposition of its "pages." Delving more intimately into the story that inspired *Le 6 Avril 1944*, it is easy to understand how this book took on the form of a box. On April 6, 1944, in the French village of Izieu, 44 Jewish children were captured by the Nazis. From there the children were deported to the death camps. The box opens to reveal, on the bottom, a photograph of a hillside and desolate house, with mirror paper bearing the names of the children surrounding it on all four sides. The effect is that the names seem eerily overlaid onto the photograph, but in fact they are two distinct elements of the work. The box helps to deliver not only a feeling of preciousness, but also confinement, and has a tomb-like quality befitting its subject.

MATERIALS AND TECHNIQUES
The handmade box is covered with Japanese paper and is blind debossed on its lid. Beneath the box's floor lies a sheet of lead to lend a tomb-like weight to the object. A silver-finished polyester delivers the mirroring effect of the walls and it is on these that the names of the children were hot-stamped in black foil.

This book was produced in an edition of 44.

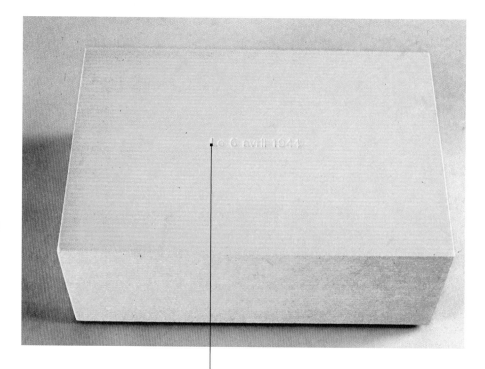

The blind-debossed title quietly announces the work

The photograph is reflected through the children's names foiled on the mirror paper

Resources and further reading

BOOKS ABOUT BOOKS

Avella, Natalie
*Paper Engineering: 3D Techniques
for 2D Materials*
Rotovision, 2006

Barton, Carol
*The Pocket Paper Engineer: How to Make
Pop-ups Step-by-step*
Popular Kinetics Press, 2005

Bodman, Sarah
Creating Artists' Books
A&C Black (UK) and Watson-Guptill
(USA), 2005

Castelman, Riva
A Century of Artists' Books
MoMA

Doggett, Sue
Handmade Books
A&C Black, 2003

Fishel, Catherine
*Mastering Materials, Bindings,
and Finishes*
Rockport, 2007

Hiner, Mark
*Paper Engineering for Pop-up Books
and Card*
Tarquin Publications, 2006

Hubert, Renee R. and Judd D.
*The Cutting Edge of Reading:
Artists' Books*
Granary Books, 1998

Lyons, Joan (Ed.)
*Artists' Books: a Critical Anthology
and Sourcebook*
Visual Studies Workshop Press, 1995

Smith, Keith A. and Jordan, Fred
Bookbinding for Book Artists
Keith A. Smith Books, 1998

Smith, Keith A.
Non-Adhesive Bindings (Volumes 1–5)
Keith A. Smith Books, 1998

Smith, Keith A.
*Structure of the Visual Book
(Expanded Edition)*
Keith A. Smith Books, 2003

Williams, Nancy
More Paperwork
Phaidon, 2005

Artists' Book Year Book (various editions)
Impact Press

WEBSITES ABOUT BOOKS, BOOK ART, AND TECHNIQUES

www.bibliopolis.net
www.boekiewoekie.com
www.bookarts.uwe.ac.uk
www.bookartbookshop.com
www.booklyn.org
www.califiabooks.com
www.centerforbookarts.com
www.designerbookbinders.org.uk
www.labookarts.com
www.petercallesen.com
www.philobiblon.com
www.popularkinetics.com
www.popupbooks.org.uk
www.sfcb.org
www.societyofbookbinders.com
www.wsworkshop.org
www.zyarts.com/zybooks

BOOKBINDING SUPPLIES, ONLINE

US
www.hollanders.com/supplies
www.philobiblon.com/suppliers.shtml
www.talas-nyc.com

UK
www.edenworkshops.com
www.falkiners.com
www.hewit.com
www.russels.com

EMBOSSING AND DEBOSSING DIE MAKERS

US
www.augustinedie.com
www.infinitystamps.com
www.owossographic.com
www.pryormarking.com

UK
www.phillips-foils.co.uk
www.sildie.com
www.studiotone.co.uk

WORKSHOPS

US
Booklyn (US)
Booklyn provides bookmaking workshops
to educators, artists, and the public
at their Brooklyn studio, and offers
internships in book production and arts
administration to university students and
adult volunteers.
www.booklyn.org

Center for Book Arts
CBA offers a range of bookbinding classes.
www.centerforbookarts.org/classes/

Hollanders
Hollanders holds a large number of workshops on bookbinding and paper arts for a range of skill levels.
www.hollanders.com/workshops

Minnesota Center for Book Arts (US)
Provides a variety of courses at different levels aimed at different groups and ages.
www.mnbookarts.org

Philobiblon
Philobiblon lists a range of course providers for bookbinding, book arts, and related programs.
www.philobiblon.com/programs.shtml

San Francisco Center for the Books
SFCB offers a very large range of workshops on binding, printing, and related arts.
www.sfcb.org/php/classes.php

Visual Studies Workshop
VSW provides a range of evening and weekend classes in bookbinding and book arts.
www.vsw.org

UK
Eden Workshops
Eden Workshops is a website with a vast array of resources, including downloadable tutorials on a number of bookbinding techniques and applications.
www.edenworkshops.com

Quay Arts
Courses in book arts and bookmaking.
www.vsw.org/education/education.html

Society of Bookbinders
The Society of Bookbinders has links on its website to a range of full- and part-time courses held within the UK.
www.societyofbookbinders.com education/education_frames.html

GRADUATE AND POSTGRADUATE COURSES

US
Mills College
Book Arts is offered as an element within undergraduate and graduate courses.
www.mills.edu/academics/undergraduate/ book/dept_courses_list.php

UK
Camberwell College of Arts
Camberwell runs an MA Book Arts program (full- and part-time) and includes Book Arts on its BA electives program.
www.camberwell.arts.ac.uk/courses/ma_ book_arts.htm

London College of Communication
LCC runs a BA (Hons) Book Arts and Design as well as shorter courses and graduate programs.
www.lcc.arts.ac.uk/courses/ undergraduate/ba_bookartscrafts.htm

University of the West of England
Book Arts is a constituent part of some undergraduate and graduate courses and there is a significant focus at The Centre for Fine Print Research.
www.uwe.ac.uk/amd

Index

Credits

Quarto would like to thank the following artists for kindly submitting images for inclusion in this book:

Mette Ambeck www.ambeck.mdd.dk: pages 112, 115
Karen Bleitz www.circlepress.com: page 108
Nicola Dale www.axisweb.org/artist/nicoladale: page 120
Daniela Deeg and Cynthia Lollis: page 107
Andrea Dezsö www.andreadezso.com: page 119
Jacques Fournier www.bibliopolis.net/roselin. Photo: Paul Litherland: page 123
Karen Hanmer www.karenhanmer.com: page 117
Rachel Hazell www.hazelldesignsbooks.co.uk: page 122
Ron King: page 111
Katsumi Komagata www.one-stroke.co.jp: page 113
Adele Outteridge: page 121
Maria G. Pisano www.philobiblon.com/guests/pisano.htm: page 118
Deb Rindl: page 116
Anne Ritz www.arbookdesign.co.uk: page 109

All other images are the copyright of Quarto Publishing plc. While every effort has been made to credit contributors, Quarto would like to apologize should there have been any omissions or errors—and would be pleased to make the appropriate correction for future editions of the book.